THE

EVERYTHING

COVER LETTER
BOOK

Great cover letters for everybody
from student to executive

Steven Graber

Adams Media Corporation
Holbrook, Massachusetts

An Everything Series Book.
The Everything Series is a trademark of Adams Media Corporation.

Published by Adams Media Corporation
260 Center Street, Holbrook, MA 02343. U.S.A.

ISBN: 1-58062-312-3

Printed in the United States of America.

J I H G F E D C B

Library of Congress Cataloging-in-Publication Data
Graber, Steven.
The everything cover letter book / by Steven Graber.
p.   cm.
Includes index.
ISBN 1-58062-312-3
1. Cover letters. I. Title.
HF5383 .G636   2000
808'.06665—dc21   99-086412

Illustrations by Barry Littmann

This book is available at quantity discounts for bulk purchases.
For information, call 1-800-872-5627.

Visit our exciting Web site at http://www.careercity.com

CONTENTS

CHAPTER THREE: THAT FINAL POLISH 41

CHAPTER FOUR: RESUMES 51

CHAPTER FIVE: ELECTRONIC RESUMES 67

CHAPTER SIX: INTERNET JOB SEARCH 83

CHAPTER NINE: CLASSIFIED ADVERTISEMENTS 145

Response to a Classified Advertisement:

CONTENTS

CONTENTS

Preface

Writing a cover letter really isn't that much different from writing a regular letter. You open with a greeting. You mention why you're writing. You close. But people get so nervous they include (or leave out) all kinds of things.

Now of course there are certain things you'll include in a cover letter that wouldn't go into a note to your mom (like the closing "Sincerely," instead of "Love,"), and this book will show you what they are. This book will also show you what to leave out as well, like any references to why your boss is such a meanie.

The Everything Cover Letter Book covers all the basics—where to put your address, the date, their address, what to say and how to say it—and a special cover letter makeover section. You'll see some common mistakes and how easily they can be corrected. And before you're ready to send off all those letters, we'll run through a checklist that will give your cover letter that final polish.

Not only does this book show you how to write an exceptional cover letter, it also includes important information on resumes, including up-to-date advice on how to write a resume that can be scanned, emailed, or posted on the Internet. And Chapter Six is something you won't find in many other job-search books—it's all about using the Internet for your job search. It includes great Web sites for you to post your resume on or to look for cool opportunities. You'll never have to leave your house to look for a job again.

And then of course comes the meat and potatoes of this book: hundreds of cover letter samples. Whether you're a cashier or an executive, a retiree or a parent re-entering the workforce, there's a sample for you. And even if you don't find an exact match for your job title or situation, take a look at some of the others. Although the jobs may be different, you just may pick up a few tips or ideas to apply to your own letter.

Remember, your cover letter has to catch the attention of the hiring manager, and there's a right way and a wrong way to do this. *The Everything Cover Letter Book* will help you do it the right way, and get your job search off on the right foot. By the time you're done reading, you really will feel like writing a cover letter is as easy as writing a note to a friend. Read on, and good luck!

PART ONE

JOB-WINNING FUNDAMENTALS

CHAPTER 1

Cover Letter Basics

Serious consideration—

Dismissal—

Your cover letter, like your resume, is a marketing tool. Too many cover letters are merely an additional piece of paper accompanying a resume, saying "Enclosed please find my resume." Like effective advertisements, effective cover letters attract an employer's attention by highlighting the most attractive features of the product. Begin by learning how to create an effective sales pitch. As with resumes, both the format and the content of your cover letter are important.

Format

Before reading a word of your cover letter, a potential employer has already made an assessment of your organizational skills and attention to detail simply by observing its appearance. How your correspondence looks to a reader can mean the difference between serious consideration and dismissal. You can't afford to settle for a less than perfect presentation of your credentials. This chapter outlines the basic format you should follow when writing a cover letter and shows you how to put the finishing touches on a top-notch product.

The Parts of a Letter

Your cover letter may be printed on the highest-quality paper and typed on a state-of-the-art computer, but if it isn't arranged according to the proper format, you won't come across as a credible candidate. Certain guidelines apply when composing any letter.

Either of two styles may be used for cover letters: business style (sometimes called block style) or personal style. The only difference between them is that in business style, all the elements of the letter—the return address, salutation, body, and complimentary close—begin at the left margin. In personal style, the return address and complimentary close begin at the centerline of the page, and paragraphs are indented.

Return Address

Your return address should appear at the top margin, without your name, either flush left or beginning at the centerline, depending on whether you re using business style or personal style. As a rule, avoid abbreviations in the addresses of your cover letter, although abbreviating the state is acceptable. Include your phone number if you re not using letterhead that contains it or it doesn t appear in the last paragraph of the letter. The idea is to make sure contact information is on both the letter and the resume, in case they get separated in the hiring manager s office (this happens more often than you would expect!).

Date

The date appears two lines below your return address, either flush left or centered, depending on which style you re using. Write out the date; don t abbreviate. *Example:* October 12, 2000.

Inside Address

Four lines beneath the date, give the addressee s full name. On subsequent lines, give the person s title, the company s name, and the company s address. Occasionally, the person s full title or the company s name and address will be very long and can appear awkward on the usual number of lines. In this case, you can use an extra line.

The text of the letter below the date should be centered approximately vertically on the page, so if your letter is short, you can begin the inside address six or even eight lines down. If the letter is long, two lines is acceptable.

Salutation

The salutation should be typed two lines beneath the company s address. It should begin Dear Mr. or Dear Ms. followed by the individual s last name and a colon. Even if you ve previously spoken with an addressee who has asked to be called by his or her first name, never use a first name in the salutation. In some

✳ Design a Letterhead

If you have a computer, you can design a letterhead for yourself and save it in a file to use for cover letters and other correspondence. Include your name, address, telephone, and e-mail, if you have it. Experiment to find an attractive design that's different from the way this information looks on your resume. If you want typefaces other than the default fonts that come with the computer, a CD-ROM containing several thousand fonts is available in software stores for about $15. However, avoid anything too flashy for business correspondence.

cases, as when responding to "blind" advertisements, a general salutation may be necessary. In such circumstances, "Dear Sir or Madam" is appropriate, followed by a colon.

Length

Three or four short paragraphs on one page is ideal. A longer letter may not be read.

Enclosure

An enclosure line is used primarily in formal or official correspondence. It's not wrong to include it in a cover letter, but it's unnecessary.

Paper Size

As with your resume, use standard 8½- by 11-inch paper. A smaller size will appear more personal than professional and is easily lost in an employer's files; a larger size will look awkward and may be discarded for not fitting with other documents.

Paper Color and Quality

Use quality paper that is standard 8½ by 11 inches and has weight and texture, in a conservative color like white or ivory. Good resume paper is easy to find at stores that sell stationery or office products and is even available at some drugstores. Use *matching* paper and envelopes for both your resume and cover letter. One hiring manager at a major magazine throws out all resumes that arrive on paper that differs in color from the envelope!

Do not buy paper with images of clouds and rainbows in the background or anything that looks like casual stationery you would send your favorite aunt. Do not spray perfume or cologne on your cover letter. Also, never use the stationery of your current employer.

Typing and Printing

Your best bet is to use a word processing program on a computer with a letter-quality printer. Handwritten letters are not acceptable. You will generally want to use the same typeface and size that you used on your resume. Remember that serif typefaces are generally easier to read.

Don't try the cheap and easy ways, like photocopying the body of your letter and typing in the inside address and salutation. Such letters will not be taken seriously.

Envelope

Mail your cover letter and resume in a standard, business-sized envelope that matches your stationery. Unless your handwriting is *extremely* neat and easy to read, type your envelopes. Address your envelope, by full name and title, specifically to the contact person you identified in your cover letter.

Content

Personalize Each Letter

If you are *not* responding to a job posting that specifies a contact name, try to determine the appropriate person to whom you should address your cover letter. (In general, the more influential the person, the better.) Try to contact the head of the department in which you're interested. This will be easiest in mid-sized and small companies, where the head of the department is likely to have an active role in the initial screening. If you're applying to a larger corporation, your application will probably be screened by the human resources department. If you're instructed to direct your inquiry to this division, try to find out the name of the senior human resources manager. This may cut down on the number of hands through which your resume passes on its way to the final decision-maker. At any rate, be sure to include your contact's name and title on both your letter and the envelope. This way, even if a new person occupies the position, your letter should get through.

Don't Philosophize

Don't:

*"Dear Ms. Sampson:
Finding the right person for the job is often difficult, costly, and at times disappointing. However, if you are in need of a reliable individual for your management staff, I have the qualifications and dedication for the position. . . ."*

Do:

*"Dear Ms. Sampson:
I would like to apply for the position of marketing manager advertised in the* Sunday Planet.*"*

Noteworthy accomplishments—

High-profit project—

Mapping It Out

A cover letter need not be longer than three or four paragraphs. Two of them, the first and last, can be as short as one sentence. The idea of the cover letter is not to repeat what's in the resume. The idea is to give an overview of your capabilities and show why you're a good candidate for the job. The best way to distinguish yourself is to highlight one or two of your accomplishments or abilities. Stressing only one or two increases your chances of being remembered.

Be sure it's clear from your letter why you have an interest in the company—*so many candidates apply for jobs with no apparent knowledge of what the company does!* This conveys the message that they just want any job. Indicating an interest doesn't mean you should tell every employer you have a burning desire to work at that company, because these statements are easy to make and invariably sound insincere. Indicating how your qualifications or experience meet their requirements may be sufficient to show why you're applying.

First paragraph. State the position for which you're applying. If you're responding to an ad or listing, mention the source. *Example:* "I would like to apply for the position of research assistant advertised in the *Sunday Planet*" (or "listed on the Internet").

Second paragraph. Indicate what you could contribute to this company and show how your qualifications will benefit them. If you're responding to an ad or listing, discuss how your skills relate to the job's requirements. Don't talk about what you can't do. Remember, keep it brief! *Example:* "In addition to my strong background in mathematics, I offer significant business experience, having worked in a data processing firm, a bookstore, and a restaurant. I am sure that my courses in statistics and computer programming would prove particularly useful in the position of trainee."

Third paragraph. If possible, show how you not only meet but exceed their requirements—why you're not just an average candidate but a superior one. Mention any noteworthy accomplishments, high-profile projects, instances where you went above and beyond the call of duty, or awards you've received for your work. If you have testimonials, commendations, or evaluations that are particularly complimentary, you may want to quote a sentence from one or two of them. *Example:* "In a letter to me, Dewayne Berry, president of NICAP Inc., said, 'Your ideas were instrumental to our success with this project.' "

Fourth paragraph. Close by saying you look forward to hearing from them. If you wish, you can also thank them for their consideration. Don't ask for an interview. If they're interested, they'll call. If not, asking won't help. Don't tell them you'll call them—many ads say "No phone calls." If you haven't heard anything in one or two weeks, a call is acceptable.

Complimentary close. The complimentary close should be two lines beneath the body of the letter, aligned with your return address and the date. Keep it simple—"Sincerely" followed by a comma, suffices. Three lines under this, type your full name as it appears on your resume. Sign above your typed name in black ink.

Don't forget to sign the letter! As silly as it sounds, people often forget this seemingly obvious detail. An oversight like this suggests you don't take care with your work. To avoid this implication if you're faxing the letter and resume directly from your computer, you can type your name directly below the complimentary close, without any intervening space. Then follow up with a hard copy of the resume and the signed letter, with your name typed in the traditional place under the signature.

Tips for Successful Cover Letters

What Writing Style Is Appropriate?

Adopt a polite, formal style that balances your confidence in yourself with respect for the employer. Keep the style clear, objective, and persuasive rather than narrative. Don't waste space boasting instead of presenting relevant qualifications.

Example: "In addition to a Bachelor of Arts degree in Business Administration, I recently received a Master's, *cum laude*, in International Marketing from Brown University. This educational experience is supported by two years' part-time experience with J&D Products, where my marketing efforts resulted in increased annual product sales of 25 percent."

Don't Be Longwinded

Don't:

"Please accept the enclosed resume as an expressed interest in contributing relevant experience to the position of Sales Representative, as advertised in the Pittsburgh Post-Gazette, *on Wednesday, April 11."*

Do:

"I would like to apply for the position of sales representative advertised in the Pittsburgh Post-Gazette.*"*

Tone: Reserved Confidence Is Always in Style

Think of how you'd sell your qualifications in a job interview. You'd probably think harder about what to say and how to say it than in an informal conversation. Above all, you'd want to sound polite, confident, and professional. Adopt a similar tone in your cover letter. It should immediately communicate confidence in your abilities. The trick is to sound enthusiastic without becoming melodramatic. Take, for example, the candidate who expressed his desire to enter the advertising field as "the single most important thing I have ever wanted in my entire twenty-three years of existence." The candidate who was actually offered the position began her letter as follows: "My extensive research into the industry, coupled with my internship and education, have confirmed my interest in pursuing an entry-level position in advertising."

Emphasize Concrete Examples

Your resume details the duties you've performed in your jobs. In contrast, your cover letter should highlight your most significant accomplishments. Instead of stating something like "My career is highlighted by several major achievements," use concrete examples:

"While Sales Manager at Shayko Chicken, I supervised a team that increased revenues by 35 percent in 18 months."

"I published four articles in *The Magical Bullet Newsletter*."

"At MUFON Corporation, I advanced from telephone fundraiser to field manager to canvassing director within two years."

List tangible, relevant skills rather than personal attributes. A sentence like "I am fluent in C++, Pascal, and COBOL" is a good substitute for a vague statement like "I am a goal-oriented, highly skilled computer programmer." Avoid using "etc."—don't expect a potential employer to imagine what else you mean. Either describe it or leave it out.

Use Powerful Language

Your language should be hard-hitting and easy to understand. Your message should be expressed using the fewest words possible.

As with your resume, make your letters interesting by using action verbs like "designed," "implemented," and "increased," rather than passive verbs like "was" and "did." Use simple, common language and avoid abbreviations and slang. Change "Responsible for directing" to "Directed" if appropriate. Also steer clear of language that's too technical or jargon-heavy. The first person who reads your cover letter may not possess the same breadth of knowledge as your future boss.

Avoid Catchphrases

In the course of a job search, it's tempting to use catch phrases you've picked up from advertisements or reference materials, phrases that sound as though they *should* go in a resume or cover letter. Many people are tempted to reach for expressions like "self-starter," "excellent interpersonal skills," and "work well independently or as part of a team."

Improve on these descriptions by listing actual projects and goals. For example, rephrase "Determined achiever with proven leadership skills" as follows: "Supervised staff of fifteen and increased the number of projects completed before deadline by 10 percent." Once you begin working, employers will discover your personal attributes for themselves. While you're under consideration, concrete experiences are more valuable than vague phrases or obscure promises.

Mention Personal Preferences?

Candidates often worry if, and how, they should include salary requirements and availability to travel or relocate. Refrain from offering salary information unless the advertisement you are responding to requires it. If you must include salary requirements, give a salary range rather than a number. Another option is to simply indicate that salary concerns are negotiable.

If you're applying to an out-of-state firm, indicate a willingness to relocate; otherwise, a hiring manager may question your purpose in writing and may not take the initiative to inquire.

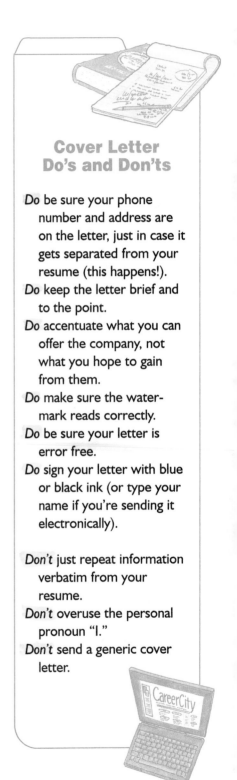

Cover Letter Do's and Don'ts

Do be sure your phone number and address are on the letter, just in case it gets separated from your resume (this happens!).

Do keep the letter brief and to the point.

Do accentuate what you can offer the company, not what you hope to gain from them.

Do make sure the watermark reads correctly.

Do be sure your letter is error free.

Do sign your letter with blue or black ink (or type your name if you're sending it electronically).

Don't just repeat information verbatim from your resume.

Don't overuse the personal pronoun "I."

Don't send a generic cover letter.

Proof with Care

Mistakes on resumes and cover letters are not only embarrassing, they will often remove you from consideration (particularly if something obvious, like your name, is misspelled). No matter how much you paid someone else to type, write, or typeset your resume or cover letter, *you* lose if there is a mistake. So proofread it as carefully as possible. Get a friend to help you. Read your draft aloud as your friend checks the proof copy. Then have your friend read aloud while you check. Next, read it letter by letter to check spelling and punctuation.

If you're having it typed or typeset by a resume service or a printer and you don't have time to proof it, pay for it and take it home. Proof it there and bring it back later to get it corrected and printed.

If you wrote your cover letter with a word processing program, use the built-in spell checker to double-check for spelling errors. Keep in mind that a spell checker will not find errors like "to" for "two" or "wok" for "work." Many spell-check programs don't recognize missing or misused punctuation, nor are they set to check the spelling of capitalized words. It's important to still proofread your cover letter for grammatical mistakes and other problems, even after it's been spell-checked.

If you find mistakes, do not fix them with pen, pencil, or white-out! Make the changes on the computer and print out the letter again.

Cover Letter Blunders to Avoid

The following discussion focuses on examples that have been adapted from real-life cover letters. Although some of these blunders may seem obvious, they occur far more often than one might think. Needless to say, none of the inquiries that included these mistakes met with positive results.

Unrelated Career Goals

Tailor your cover letter to the position you're applying for. A hiring manager is only interested in what you can do for the company, not what you hope to accomplish for yourself. Convey a genuine interest in the position and a long-term pledge to fulfilling its duties. *Don't*

Example A (wrong way): "While my true goal is to become a professional dancer, I am exploring the option of taking on proofreading work while continuing to train for the Boston Ballet's next audition." *Do*

Example B (right way): "I am very interested in this proofreading position, and I am confident of my ability to make a long-term contribution to your capable staff."

Comparisons and Clichés

Avoid clichés and obvious comparisons. These expressions detract from your letter's purpose: to highlight your most impressive skills and accomplishments.

Examples of what not to do:

"My word processor runs like the wind."

"I am a people person."

"Teamwork is my middle name."

"Your company is known as the crème de la crème of accounting firms."

"I am as smart as a whip."

"Among the responses you receive for this position, I hope my qualifications make me leader of the pack."

Wasted Space

Since cover letters are generally four paragraphs long, every word of every sentence should be directly related to your purpose for writing. In other words, if you are applying for a position as a chemist, include only those skills and experiences most applicable to that field. Any other information weakens your application.

Examples of what not to do:

"As my enclosed resume reveals, I possess the technical experience and educational background to succeed as your newest civil engineer. In addition, I am a certified gymnastics instructor who has won several local competitions."

"I am writing in response to your advertisement for an accounting clerk. Currently, I am finishing an associate degree at

✳ Next Candidate, Please

Certain formats and phrases signal an employer that you're using a form letter. Some job candidates turn this blunder into an art. In one real-life example, a candidate created a form letter with blank spaces where he penned in the employer's name and position applied for.

Another applicant who was indecisive about her field of interest created a list of possible positions in her letter. She then circled the most appropriate job description, depending on the company.

Peacock Junior College. My courses have included medieval architecture, film theory, basic home surgery, and nutrition."

Form Letters

Mass mailings, in which you send a form letter to a large number of employers, are not recommended. This approach doesn't allow you to personalize each application. Every cover letter you write should be tailored to the position you're seeking and should demonstrate your commitment to a specific industry and familiarity with each employer. Mass mailings may indicate to a hiring manager that you're not truly interested in joining that organization.

Inappropriate Stationery

White and ivory are the only acceptable paper colors for a cover letter. Also, don't rely on graphics to "improve" your cover letter; let your qualifications speak for themselves. If you're a cat enthusiast, don't use stationery with images of favorite felines. If you're a musician, don't send a letter decorated with a border of musical notes and instruments.

"Amusing" Anecdotes

Imagine yourself in an interview setting. Since you don't know your interviewer, you wouldn't joke with him or her until you determined what demeanor was appropriate. Similarly, when writing, remain polite and professional.

Erroneous Company Information

If you were the employer, would you want to hire a candidate who confuses your company's products and services or misquotes recent activities? To avoid such errors, verify the accuracy of any company information you mention in your cover letter. On the other hand, if you haven't researched the company, don't bluff. Statements like "I know something about your company" or "I am familiar with your products" signal to an employer that you haven't done your homework.

Desperation

In your cover letter, sound determined, not desperate. While an employer appreciates enthusiasm, he or she may be turned off by a desperate plea for employment. However, a fine line often separates the two.

Examples of what not to do:

"I am desperately eager to start, as I have been out of work for six months."

"Please call today! I'll be waiting by the phone."

"I really, really need this job to pay off medical bills."

"I AM VERY BADLY IN NEED OF MONEY!"

Personal Photos

Unless you're seeking employment in modeling, acting, or other performing arts, it's inappropriate to send a photograph.

Confessed Shortcomings

Some job seekers mistakenly call attention to their weaknesses in their cover letters, hoping to ward off an employer's objections. This is a mistake, because the letter emphasizes your flaws rather than your strengths.

Examples of what not to do:

"Although I have no related experience, I remain very interested in the management consultant position."

"I may not be well qualified for this position, but it has always been my dream to work in the publishing field."

Misrepresentation

In any stage of the job-search process, never, *ever*, misrepresent yourself. In many companies, erroneous information contained in a cover letter or resume will be grounds for dismissal if the inaccuracy is discovered. Protect yourself by sticking to the facts. You're selling your skills and accomplishments in your cover letter. If you achieve something, say so, and put it in the best possible light. Don't hold back or be modest—no one else will. At the same time, don't exaggerate to the point of misrepresentation.

Don't Be Grandiose

Don't:

"As a recent graduate of Mitzelflick University with a degree in Biology, I am currently launching my career as an environmental campaigner in hopes of reversing global warming and ozone depletion on a world-wide basis. . . ."

Do:

"I would like to apply for the position of environmental campaigner due to my strong interest in many environmental causes."

Gimmicks -

Examples of what not to do:

"In June, I graduated with honors from American University. In the course of my studies, I played two varsity sports while concurrently holding five jobs."

"Since beginning my career four years ago, I have won hundreds of competitions and awards and am considered by many to be the best hairstylist on the east coast."

Demanding Statements

Your cover letter should demonstrate what you can do for an employer, not what he or she can do for you. For example, instead of stating "I am looking for a unique opportunity in which I will be adequately challenged and compensated," say "I am confident I could make a significant contribution to your organization, specifically by expanding your customer base in the northwest and instituting a discount offer for new accounts." Also, since you're requesting an employer's consideration, your letter shouldn't include personal preferences or demands. Statements like "It would be an overwhelmingly smart idea for you to hire me" or "Let's meet next Wednesday at 4:00 P.M., when I will be available to discuss my candidacy further" come across as presumptuous. Job candidates' demands are rarely met with an enthusiastic response.

Missing Resume

Have you ever forgotten to enclose all the materials you refer to in your cover letter? This is a fatal oversight. No employer is going to take the time to remind you of your mistake; he or she has already moved on to the next application.

Personal Information

Do not include your age, health, physical characteristics, marital status, race, religion, political/moral beliefs, or any other personal information. List your personal interests and hobbies only if they're directly relevant to the type of job you're seeking. If you're applying to a company that greatly values teamwork, for instance, citing that you organized a community fundraiser or played on a

basketball team may be advantageous. When in doubt, however, leave it out.

Choice of Pronouns

Your cover letter necessarily requires a thorough discussion of your qualifications. Although some applicants might choose the third person ("he or she") as a creative approach to presenting their qualifications, potential employers sometimes find this disconcerting. In general, using the first person ("I") is preferable.

Example A (wrong way): "Bambi Berenbeam is a highly qualified public relations executive with over seven years of relevant experience in the field. She possesses strong verbal and written communication skills, and has an extensive client base."

Example B (right way): "I am a highly qualified public relations executive with over seven years of relevant experience in the field. I possess strong verbal and written communication skills and have an extensive client base."

Tone Trouble

Tone problems are subtle and may be hard to detect. When reading your cover letter, patrol for tone problems by asking yourself, after each sentence, "Does this statement enhance my candidacy? Could a hiring manager interpret it in an unfavorable way?" Have a second reader review your letter. If the letter's wording is questionable, rewrite it. A cover letter should steer a middle course between extremely formal, which can come across as pretentious, and extremely informal, which can come across as presumptuous. Try to sound genuine, not stilted. When in doubt, err on the side of formality.

Gimmicks

Gimmicks like sending a home video or a singing telegram to replace the conventional cover letter may seem attractive. No matter how creative these ideas may sound, the majority of employers will be more impressed with a simple, well-crafted letter. In the worst-case scenario, gimmicks can even work against

---

Details, Details . . .

Can and May

No: *I may be reached at (505) 555-5555 (days) and (505) 444-4444 (evenings).*

Better: *I can be reached at (505) 555-5555 (days) and (505) 444-4444 (evenings).*

Fused Participle

No: *I appreciate you taking the time to speak to me is an example of a fused participle and is grammatically incorrect.*

Better: *I appreciate **your** taking the time to speak to me.*

Serial Comma

Standard editorial practice in a series of items is to use a comma after each item except the last.

No: *" . . . lumberjack, lounge lizard and organ grinder."*

Yes: *" . . . lumberjack, lounge lizard, and organ grinder."*

Special situations = special skills —
e.g.: Running marathons or cooking foods (in home)

you, eliminating you from consideration. Examples include sending a poster-sized cover letter by courier service or a baseball hat with a note attached: "I'm throwing my hat into the ring!" Avoid such big risks; most hiring decisions are based on qualifications, not gimmicks.

Typographical Errors

It's easy to make mistakes in your letters, particularly when you're writing many in succession. But it's also easy for a hiring manager to reject any cover letter that contains errors, even those that seem minor. Don't make the mistake that one job-hunting editor made, citing his attention to detail while misspelling his own name! Here are a few common technical mistakes to watch out for when proofreading your letter:

Misspelling the hiring contact's name or title in the address or salutation or on the envelope.

Forgetting to change the name of the organization you're applying to each time it appears in your application, especially in the body of the letter. For example, if you're applying to Boots and Bags, don't express enthusiasm for a position at Shoe City.

Indicating application for one position and mentioning a different position in the body of the letter. For instance, one candidate applying for a telemarketing position included the following statement: "I possess fifteen years experience related to the marketing analyst opening." Another mistake here is that the applicant didn't use "years" as a possessive: "... fifteen years' experience...."

Messy Corrections

Your cover letter should contain *all* pertinent information. If, for any reason, you forget to communicate something to your addressee, retype the letter. Including a supplementary note, either typed or handwritten, will be viewed as unprofessional or, worse, lazy. For example, one candidate attached a "post-it" note to his cover letter, stating his willingness to travel and/or relocate. This and all other information must be included in your final draft. Also, avoid using correction fluid or penning in any corrections.

Omitted Signature

However obvious this may sound, don't forget to sign your name neatly in blue or black ink. Far too many letters have a typed name but no signature. Also, don't use a script font or a draw program on your word processor.

Cover Letters for Special Situations

Writing a cover letter can seem like an even more formidable task when you find yourself in what we call "special situations." Perhaps you lack paid job experience, have been out of the workplace to raise children, are concerned about possible discrimination due to age or disability, or are trying to enter a field in which you have no practical experience. The key to improving your cover letter in these special situations is to emphasize your strengths. Focus on your marketable skills (whether they were acquired in the workplace or elsewhere), and highlight impressive achievements, relevant education and training, and/or related interests. And, of course, you should take care to downplay or eliminate any information that may be construed as a weakness.

For example, if you're a "displaced homemaker" (a homemaker entering the job market for the first time), you can structure your cover letter to highlight the special skills you've acquired over the years while downplaying your lack of paid experience. If you're an older job candidate, use your age as a selling point. Emphasize the depth of your experience, your maturity, your sense of responsibility, and your positive outlook. Changing careers? Instead of focusing on your job history, emphasize the marketable skills you've acquired that are considered valuable in the position you're seeking. For example, let's say your career has been real estate and, in your spare time, you like to run marathons. Recently, you heard about an opening in the sales and marketing department at an athletic shoe manufacturer. What you need to do is emphasize the skills you have that the employer is looking for. Not only do you have strong sales experience, you're familiar with the needs of the company's market, and that's a powerful combination!

The Comedian and the Chemist

Tone may vary somewhat according to profession: a comedian and a chemist would choose dissimilar tones. While it would be perfectly fitting for a comedian to adopt a lighthearted, familiar tone, the chemist would be best served by a more formal voice. Err on the side of caution, for there may be a lot of comedians out there, but there aren't many applying to be one.

Response to a "Blind" Advertisement

A form of classified advertisements, "Blind" advertisements do not list employer information and generally direct inquiries to a post office box rather than a company's address. Since you're not provided with a company name in a blind ad, your cover letter should sharply define your knowledge of the industry, position (if mentioned) and how your qualifications specifically match up to the stated requirements. In other words, tailor your letter to any information given. For example, consider a blind ad that reads:

Large-size law firm in need of paralegal with experience in legal research, writing briefs, and office administration.

You need to target everything in your response: what you know of the operations of large-size firms; why you want to be and remain a paralegal; how much experience you have in legal research and writing; and exactly what office skills you have. Avoid longwinded passages that don't follow these guidelines. Without knowing your readers, you've caught their attention. They're more likely to invite you for an interview, and suddenly you're one step closer to getting the job.

Cold Letters

With a "cold" cover letter, you can directly contact potential employers without a referral or previous correspondence. Jobseekers most commonly use this type of letter to advertise their availability to hiring managers or personnel departments. Presumably, after researching your field, you will have devised a list of the top employers you would like to work for and gathered basic company information for each.

Broadcast Letters

With a broadcast letter, well-qualified candidates can advertise their availibility to top-level professionals in a particular field. The candi-

date attempts to entice the potential employer to consider his or her impressive qualifications for available positions. Although the broadcast letter discusses a candidate's background in detail, a resume is usually included. Since this type of letter is used primarily by seasoned executives, its tone should reflect the candidate's experience, knowledge, and confidence in his or her capabilities.

A candidate using the broadcast letter format might begin, "Are you in need of a management accountant who, in her most recent association, contributed to productivity improvements resulting in an annual savings of $20 million?" This attention-grabbing opening is effective only if the reader understands the significance of such an accomplishment. For this reason, broadcast letters are not recommended for those candidates conducting widespread job searches, where cover letters may end up in the human resources department rather than in the hands of a fellow industry executive.

Letter to an Employment Agency

When searching for a job, many candidates rely on the help of employment agencies. These agencies offer services to a wide range of job-seekers, primarily for clerical or support staff positions. Letters addressed to employment agencies should focus on who you are, what type of position you are looking for and in what specific industry, and some of your strongest skills related to that field. For the agency to place you in an appropriate position, mention personal preferences, including geographic and salary requirements.

Letter to an Executive Search Firm

Although executive search firms actively recruit candidates for client companies, don't let this discourage you from writing. A well-crafted cover letter can alert an otherwise unknowing recruiter to your availability. Highlight your most impressive accomplishments and attributes and briefly summarize all relevant experience. If you have

✳ Don't Give Your Life Story

Don't:

"Six years ago, I started a career in nursing. I subsequently left to manage the division of a company and later resigned from this lucrative position to pursue my first career, nursing."

Do:

"I have several years' nursing experience and significant business management experience. I am sure that this background would make me well qualified for the Nursing Home Director position."

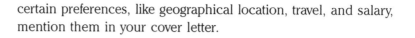

certain preferences, like geographical location, travel, and salary, mention them in your cover letter.

Networking Letters

For the most part, networking letters refer to a third-party industry contact to garner the reader's attention and induce him or her to assist you in your job search. It is essential to achieve the right tone in your networking letters. Unless you are familiar with a contact, word your correspondence in a businesslike manner. In other words, do not use your addressee's first name or rely on an overly casual writing style. Likewise, if you have been in contact with this person recently, it could be useful to remind him or her, "It was great seeing you at the Chicago Writers' Convention last month" or "It's been several months since we bumped into each other on that flight to London. How are you?"

Many networking letters are written to an addressee whom the candidate has not met but has been referred to by a mutual acquaintance. In this case, immediately state the name of the person who referred you, such as "Jean Rawlins suggested I contact you." It is generally more effective to ask a contact with whom you are unfamiliar for assistance and names of people to contact than it is to ask for a job. Chances are, if your letter is politely persuasive, people will be interested in talking with you.

Thank You Letters

Your correspondence doesn't end with cover letters. Other types of letters, such as thank you letters, are often appropriate, even obligatory. It's acceptable to handwrite your thank you letter on a generic blank note card (but *never* a postcard). Make sure handwritten notes are neat and legible. If you're in doubt, typing your letter is always a safe bet. If you met with several people, it's fine to send each an individual thank you letter. Call the company if you need to check on the correct spelling of their names. Remember to keep the letters short, proofread them carefully, and send them *promptly*.

After a Telephone Conversation

Immediately after a telephone conversation with a potential employer, send a cover letter expressing your gratitude for his or her time. Use this opportunity to reiterate your qualifications and continued interest in the position. Be sure to include your resume.

After a Job Interview

Always send a thank you letter after an interview, ideally within twenty-four hours. So few candidates do this, yet it's another way for you to stand out. A follow-up letter expresses thanks for the employer's time and emphasizes your continued interest in the position. It can also provide a convenient opportunity to reiterate your unique qualifications.

Mention something specific from the interview and restate your interest in the company and the position. As with resumes and cover letters, avoid catch phrases, and be careful the letter doesn't come across sounding canned or hypocritical. Don't say, for example, "I would like to reiterate my strong interest in this position. I believe it would be an exciting opportunity, and I feel that my track record shows I would be a successful candidate." The letter should be brief (no more than a page; even a few sentences is fine) and personalized.

For a Good Reference

During the course of your job search, it may be necessary to call upon personal and professional references to support your credentials. These people are doing you a favor and deserve your written thanks. Thank you letters also allow you to keep your contacts current.

When writing your letter, you might want to remind the person why you needed the reference and the outcome of his or her efforts. Keep your comments brief and your tone polite.

For a Letter of Recommendation

Potential employers sometimes require letters of recommendation. These may be written by previous employers or, for those with

✕ More Cover Letter Don'ts

Following are some actual real-life examples, sent by job seekers, that illustrate what NOT to write in your cover letter:

"I am excited by the prospect of growing with [BLANK SPACE] and look forward to discussing your needs."

"Marketing is in my blood, and I believe that I am genetically predetermined to enter the marketing world . . . I am writing to you about possible job openings in your company in hopes that I can fulfill my destiny there."

"As my resume indicates, I have extensive experience in pubic relations."

Informational interview—

little professional experience, by college professors. Since you requested this person's time, it's only courteous to express your written thanks. By doing so, the person will be more likely to remember you should you require further assistance in the future.

For a Referral

Many jobs are found with the assistance of a networking contact or referral. Throughout your job search, keep track of all your referrals and send each one a personalized thank you note. Briefly express sincere gratitude for the referral's help on your behalf. If the person's efforts directly led to a positive outcome for you, let him or her know. It may be advantageous to offer your return assistance. In any event, sending a thoughtful thank you letter is an invaluable career move. If you recognize someone's assistance on your behalf, the person may be more likely to help you again in the future.

After an Informational Interview

Thank you letters aren't restricted to potential employers. Everyone who assists you in any way during the course of your job search deserves written thanks. Even in the case of an informational interview, a letter is required. Although you're not asking for a job, you've taken a person's time and should thank him or her accordingly.

Consider Susan, who wrote a timely thank you letter to an industry executive with whom she met in an informational interview. The executive, impressed by her considerate attention to detail, heard about an appropriate employment opportunity several weeks later and recommended her for the job.

Resurrection Letter

If several weeks or even months have passed since you mailed your initial inquiry and you haven't received a response, your candidacy may be in need of a jump start. Sending a resurrection letter informs an employer of your continued interest in, and suitability for, a desired position. Begin by reminding the employer of your initial reason for writing. Next, reiterate your most relevant qualifications and stress your desire to join the employer's organization. Be sure to close your letter by clearly stating how and when you can be reached, and enclose another resume for the employer's convenience.

Waiting for a response to your application can be frustrating. If you feel this way, don't let it show in your resurrection letter. A hiring manager is more likely to respond to a polite, upbeat letter.

Response to Rejection

A well-written thank you note, mailed within one or two days of receiving notice of rejection, makes a positive statement. Admittedly, this technique is less widely used than other thank you letters, but it can be equally effective.

When writing your letter, emphasize an interest in being considered for future openings. Also, be careful to use an upbeat tone. Although you may be disappointed, you don't want to imply that you don't respect the employer's hiring decision.

Withdrawal from Consideration

If you must withdraw your application from consideration at any point in the hiring process, it's best to inform the employer in writing. This will establish you as a courteous individual worthy of consideration should you reapply for a position in the future. In general, a withdrawal letter should be concise. If you choose to include a reason for your withdrawal, phrase it briefly and in positive terms.

Rejection of an Offer

If you decide to reject an employment offer, inform the employer through a formal letter. Even if you rejected the offer over the phone, confirm your decision in writing. Begin by thanking the interviewer for both the offer and the time extended to your candidacy. Stating a reason for rejection is optional. Above

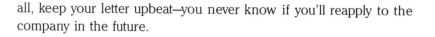

all, keep your letter upbeat—you never know if you'll reapply to the company in the future.

Acceptance Letter

Even if you've been offered the position of your choice, no hiring decision is final until it's in writing. Confirm your acceptance of a job offer with a brief, gracious letter. Express thanks for the organization's decision and your enthusiasm for the new position.

Address or Telephone Number Change

In today's tough market, the job-search process is often lengthy. If your situation has changed since your last correspondence (i.e., a geographical move or phone number change), always inform a potential employer. Keep your correspondence brief. This is a courtesy letter, not a full-page reiteration of your qualifications.

To begin, remind the employer of the position you applied for, and when. State the change in your circumstances and thank the reader for his or her continued consideration. Include an updated copy of your resume. Remember that this letter is not optional. An employer will not waste time trying to track you down.

Resignation Letter

Always send a formal resignation letter at least two weeks before terminating your present employment. Many resignation letters simply state your last day of employment and a willingness to assist in the transition process. Other letters may personally thank the employer and/or explain your reasons for departure. Whatever the circumstances, phrase your resignation letter in a positive way. Your past employer might be called on to provide a reference for you in the future.

CHAPTER 2

Cover Letter Makeovers

This chapter contains six cover letter makeovers, to give you an idea of what goes into improving a less than outstanding cover letter. Each one is shown in a "Before" version, with an analysis of its shortcomings, followed by an "After" version.

Before

- ✖ Don't just repeat information in your resume.

- ✖ Don't congratulate them on their success.

- ✖ Don't repeat the person's name in the body of the letter—it sounds phony.

178 Green Street
Daytona Beach, FL 32115
(904) 555-5555

August 18, 2001

Pat Cummings
Hiring Manager
Any Advertising Agency
1140 Main Street
Orlando, FL 32816

Dear Mr. Cummings:

I am very interested in pursuing my career in the advertising industry at Any Advertising Agency. While researching area firms, I read an exciting piece in *Ad World* about your recent campaign for Homeloving soups. Congratulations on receiving a Cleo Award for your efforts!

I would love to join your winning team in an entry-level, administrative position. I can offer over eight years' of administration, promotion, and communication experience. The following achievements would be especially beneficial to your firm:

Administration: Recordkeeping and file maintenance. Data processing and computer operations, accounts receivable, accounts payable, accounting research and reports. Order fulfillment, inventory control, and customer relations. Scheduling, office management, and telephone reception.

Promotion: Composing, editing, and proofreading correspondence and PR materials for own house cleaning service.

Communication: Instruction, curriculum and lesson planning, student evaluation, parent-teacher conferences, development of educational materials. Training and supervising clerks.

Computer Skills: Proficient in Microsoft Word, Lotus 1-2-3, Excel, Filemaker Pro, and ADDS Accounting System.

I would like to request a personal interview to further outline my skills, and how they could be immediately applicable to an administrative position at Any Advertising Agency. I will call your office on August 23 to schedule a convenient meeting time.

Thank you, Mr. Cummings. I look forward to our conversation.

Sincerely,

Chris Smith

Chris Smith

CAREER CHANGER
Advertising Assistant

178 Green Street
Daytona Beach, FL 32115
(904) 555-5555

August 18, 2001

Pat Cummings
Hiring Manager
Any Advertising Agency
1140 Main Street
Orlando, FL 32816

Dear Mr. Cummings:

I would like to inquire about the possibility of a position at your agency. I have over eight years' experience in promotion, communications, and administration.

As owner of a housecleaning service for four years, I designed and wrote all promotional materials, including direct-mail coupons. Immediately after my first promotional campaign, the volume of business tripled, resulting in my hiring six people. In addition to supervising the employees, I managed the office, which entailed handling calls, scheduling, billing, record keeping, ordering supplies, and customer relations. I found that what I enjoyed most was promotion, so I have just sold the business and am seeking a position in advertising.

In addition to my business experience, I have strong communication skills from prior employment as a teacher, which enables me to explain ideas clearly. These skills also enabled me to procure donations of computers and software from a local business and to promote school fundraising events.

I hope to hear from you if you have an opening for someone with my qualifications.

Thank you for your consideration.

Sincerely,

Chris Smith

Chris Smith

✔ Even if you switch careers, you want to present a consistent message—here it's on her communication skills.

✔ The reference to "entry-level" is too restrictive because her skills may qualify her for a higher level job, so it's been deleted.

RESPONSE TO A "BLIND" ADVERTISEMENT
Legal Associate

Before

* First sentence is confusing—did this person really receive both degrees recently?

* How can a person be anxious to join a firm when responding to a blind ad?

* Don't describe your enclosed resume—people know what it is.

178 Green Street
Alfred, NY 14802
(607) 555-5555

October 28, 2001

P.O. Box 7777
Conway, SC 29526

Re: Legal Associate

Dear Sir/Madam:

In addition to a Juris Doctor degree, I recently received a Master of Law in Banks and Banking Law Studies with a concentration in International Law. I am looking for the opportunity to join the legal staff of a bank or corporation where I can put my experience in general legal practice and recent graduate degree to practical use and further develop my legal capabilities.

My expertise is in the supervision of associate and support legal staff in all phases of research, document preparation, and coordination as required for all legal issues. I am well organized, accurate, and conscientious, interface well with individuals and groups, and feel confident that I can be a contributing asset to your firm.

I am most anxious to become a part of your firm and would appreciate meeting with you at your convenience. The enclosed resume is a brief summary of my academic accomplishments and work experience.

I look forward to your response.

Sincerely,

Chris Smith

Chris Smith

RESPONSE TO A "BLIND" ADVERTISEMENT
Legal Associate

178 Green Street
Alfred, NY 14802
(607) 555-5555

October 28, 2001

P.O. Box 7777
Conway, SC 29526

Dear Sir or Madam:

I would like to apply for the legal associate position advertised in *Lawyers Weekly*. As you will note from my resume, I hold a Juris Doctor degree and recently received a Master of Law in Banks and Banking Law Studies, with a concentration in International Law.

Aside from familiarity with all phases of research, document preparation, and coordination, I have experience supervising associate and support legal staff. One case I worked on for the defense was *Acme v. Smith*. After the surprise decision for the defense, Jack Robinson, the defense co-counsel, sent me a letter in which he said, "I want to thank you for your significant contribution to a well-prepared case."

I also have experience with maritime issues and international law pertaining to shipping. I have dealt with several foreign shipping lines regarding bulk transport of oil, grain, and other commodities, as well as customs procedures and matters involving the Coast Guard.

If my qualifications meet your needs, I hope you will give me the opportunity to speak to you further about the available position.

Sincerely,

Chris Smith

Chris Smith

✔ Mention where you saw the ad.

✔ This version mentions specific accomplishments rather than generic statements.

Before

* The second, fourth, and fifth paragraphs are generic, bland, and unnecessary.

* The third paragraph lacks organization. It should be in either chronological order or order of importance.

178 Green Street
Newport, RI 02840
May 14, 2001

Search Committee
P.O. Box 7777
Providence, RI 02908

RE: Sixth Grade Teaching Position

Dear Search Committee:

I have enclosed my resume in response to your advertisement in the May edition of *Education in New England.*

During the past several years, I have been preparing myself for a position as a teacher in an established school system, where I can apply my teaching, training, and administrative experience to manage and motivate a classroom of students toward higher education.

As a Student Teacher with the Easton Public School System, I successfully taught literature, public speaking, and creative writing at the secondary level. I received my bachelor's degree and certification in Elementary Education in 1999 from Stonehill College in Easton, Massachusetts. Also, I have acted as a Substitute Teacher in several school districts over a four-year period and have designed, organized, and taught my own summer course for gifted children in the town of Newport for the past two years.

Currently, I am seeking an opportunity with a system that offers continued professional development and the opportunity for advancement in the field of education. I would welcome a personal interview to discuss in detail my ability to handle the teaching position and my compatibility with the rest of your staff.

In the interim, should you require additional information, please contact me at the above address or by phone at (401) 555-5555.

Yours sincerely,

Chris Smith

Chris Smith

RESPONSE TO A "BLIND" ADVERTISEMENT
Teacher

178 Green Street
Newport, RI 02840
(401) 555-5555

May 14, 2001

Search Committee
P.O. Box 7777
Providence, RI 02908

Dear Sirs and Ladies:

I would like to apply for the position of sixth-grade teacher advertised in *Education in New England.*

I hold a bachelor's degree and certification in Elementary Education. As a student teacher with the Easton public school system, I taught literature, public speaking, and creative writing at the secondary level.

For the past four years, I have acted as a substitute teacher in several school districts. I am pleased to be able to say that a number of teachers have told me they ask for me as a substitute, because I continue their lesson plans rather than giving the students a study hall. The students are also pleased with the techniques I use for different learning styles—visual, auditory, tactile, and kinesthetic. Even though some students may not have an obvious learning problem, a number of them have said they find it easier to learn using one of the alternative techniques.

My interest in new learning styles motivated me to design and teach my own course for gifted children in Newport during the past two summers. Although the parents were accustomed to their children's accomplishments, even they were surprised at the progress the students made in just six weeks.

I greatly enjoy teaching and hope you will give me the opportunity to discuss the available position with you further.

Thank you for your consideration.

Yours sincerely,

Chris Smith

Chris Smith

✔ Don't forget to specifically mention to which job you are applying. Companies may have multiple ads in the same newspaper.

✔ The third and fourth paragraphs now mention specific accomplishments that help define this candidate.

"COLD" LETTER TO A POTENTIAL EMPLOYER
Elementary School Teacher

Before

✖ This candidate fails to mention specific accomplishments.

✖ Since this person is from out of state, she should mention that she is relocating to the area to clarify why she's looking for a new job.

178 Green Street
Lubbock, TX 79408
(806) 555-5555

July 7, 2001

Pat Cummings, Ph.D.
Superintendent
Any Public School
1140 Main Street
Chickasha, OK 73023

Dear Dr. Cummings:

My interest in contributing to the enhancement of elementary education within the Any Public School System has prompted my forwarding the enclosed resume for your review and consideration.

Currently, as an Elementary School Teacher responsible for thirty second-grade students, I am actively involved in the development and implementation of reading, writing, and math programs which effectively motivate accomplishment through both individual and group projects. My professional training and experience began with the Rockford Public School System as a Student Teacher at the Roosevelt Elementary School and as a Substitute Teacher within the system. I completed a Bachelor of Arts in Elementary Education in May 1992.

Additionally, I have been instrumental in instituting and selecting educational software for a new computer system as well as instructing the teaching staff on its use. Presently, I am formulating a proposal to initiate the establishment of a high-ability learning program.

I am confident of my ability to stimulate and motivate children toward personal growth and achievement. I would welcome the opportunity to meet with you to discuss your current staffing requirements. In the interim, if any additional information is required, please contact me at the above address or phone number.

Sincerely,

Chris Smith

Chris Smith

"COLD" LETTER TO A POTENTIAL EMPLOYER
Elementary School Teacher

178 Green Street
Lubbock, TX 79408
(806) 555-5555

July 7, 2001

Pat Cummings, Ph.D.
Superintendent
Any Public School
1140 Main Street
Chickasha, OK 73023

Dear Dr. Cummings:

I will be relocating to Chickasha this summer and would like to inquire about elementary teaching positions for September in the Any Public School system.

As you will note from my resume, I hold a Bachelor of Arts in Elementary Education. My professional training and experience began with the Rockford public school system, as a student teacher and substitute teacher. I have been employed as a fourth-grade teacher at Franklin Elementary School in Lubbock, where one of my projects was formulating a proposal for a high-ability learning program. The program was subsequently implemented, showed impressive results, and received favorable comment from both parents and students. Enclosed is an article I wrote describing the program that appeared in *Elementary Education* last August.

While at Franklin, I also took primary responsibility for selecting educational software for a new computer system and instructing the teaching staff in its use. The computers turned out to be a big hit with students, who took every opportunity to use them and the software. Again, parents were pleased with the improvement their children showed.

I look forward to hearing from you if you have an opening for someone with my qualifications.

Thank you for your consideration.

Sincerely,

Chris Smith

Chris Smith

After

✔ The first paragraph now clarifies why this person is applying.

✔ The third and fourth paragraphs help define why this person is a superior candidate by mentioning highlights in her career.

Before

- ✖ Ask not what the company can do for you, but rather what you can do for the company—this opening sounds very self-absorbed.

- ✖ "Prestigious organization" sounds phony as does "it would be an honor."

- ✖ This letter is too short and generic.

1221 Oak Garden Road
Brookline, MA 02351
(617) 555-8850

April 1, 2000

Mr. Shawn Belleau, Director
WGUR TV-Channel 46
133 Business Park Drive
Brighton, MA 02215

Dear Mr. Belleau:

I am contacting you to see if you have any openings where I can continue to grow and learn.

I am presently studying Communications at Emerson College and will be graduating next month. I have taken many communications courses that I think would help me be a good fit with your prestigious organization. I also have television experience as a program intern for a call-in show.

It would be an honor to interview with your company. You may call me at the above number.

Sincerely,

Chris Smith

Chris Smith

STUDENT
Communications Major

1221 Oak Garden Road
Brookline, MA 02351
(617) 555-8850

April 1, 2000

Mr. Shawn Belleau, Director
WGUR TV-Channel 46
133 Business Park Drive
Brighton, MA 02215

Dear Mr. Belleau:

    Sharon Lafferty, director of the "A.M. Boston" program suggested that I contact you regarding an opening you may have for a Production Assistant.

    I am presently studying Communications at Emerson College and will be graduating next month. My course work is concentrated in Broadcast Journalism and I have studied such topics as Ethics in Reporting, Broadcast Journalism I-IV, and Television Production. I was the top student in my Broadcast Journalism classes and was consistently recognized for academic excellence on the Dean's List.

    I also have experience working in television, having worked as a Television Program Intern for "A.M. Boston." Here, I was responsible for booking guests to debate controversial public interest topics with the host and fielding viewers' reaction calls provoked by on-air debates. Also, I gained valuable experience assembling and editing video clips of upcoming entertainment events and movies which were aired during the show.

    I would value the opportunity to meet with you to discuss a possible position with your station. I can be reached at the above address and telephone number.

    Thank you for your time.

Sincerely,

Chris Smith

Chris Smith

After

✔ Be more specific about what type of job you want without painting yourself into a corner with restrictive clauses like "entry-level."

✔ Note specific academic achievements that make this candidate stand out.

✔ The television experience is explained in better detail here.

Before

* The main paragraph is generic and bland.

* Never bad-mouth a boss!

* Your reasons for leaving should not focus on problems you have with other people.

* In general, you shouldn't mention that you'll call them and certainly not in such a phony way as this.

178 Green Street
Ecru, MS 38842
(601) 555-5555
November 1, 2000

Pat Cummings
Office Manager
Any Corporation
1140 Main Street
Chicago, IL 60605

Dear Mr. Cummings:

Your advertisement in the *Jackson Review* calls for an assistant with a background in a variety of administrative skills, such as mine.

As an administrative assistant at Lambert Hospital, I was in charge of all computer support, word processing, and database, spreadsheet, and administrative functions. My duties included purchasing, equipment maintenance, daily office operations, supervising staff and volunteers, and coordinating various projects with staff and outside vendors. I'm leaving this position because my current boss doesn't appreciate all my efforts.

I will call you on Thursday to discuss what a superior candidate I am!

Sincerely,

Chris Smith

Chris Smith

RESPONSE TO A CLASSIFIED ADVERTISEMENT
Administrative Assistant

178 Green Street
Ecru, MS 38842
(601) 555-5555
November 1, 2001

Pat Cummings
Office Manager
Any Corporation
1140 Main Street
Chicago, IL 60605

Dear Mr. Cummings:

I am applying for the position of administrative assistant as advertised in the *Jackson Review*.

As an administrative assistant at Lambert Hospital, I was in charge of all computer support, word processing, and database, spreadsheet, and administrative functions for the admissions department. My last supervisor commented that I was instrumental in making the installation of a hospital-wide computer network a smooth one.

In addition to my administrative skills, I also have experience in training and supervising new personnel and volunteers. This August, I was responsible for hiring and training two temporary workers to cover a staffing shortage.

I look forward to discussing this position with you. Feel free to contact me at the above phone number.

Thank you very much for you time.

Sincerely,

Chris Smith

Chris Smith

✔ This opening is more straightforward and professional.

✔ The main paragraphs are more specific and the reference to a personality conflict with the boss has been deleted.

✔ The closing is more professional as well.

CHAPTER 3

That Final Polish

This chapter contains a list of details, often overlooked, that will give your cover letter that final polish.

Format
Apostrophe

A common mistake is to refer to "over five years experience in the field." *Years* here is a type of possessive (technically a *descriptive genitive*) and must have an apostrophe: *five years' experience.*

Cum Laude

Cum laude, magna cum laude, and summa cum laude are lowercase and italic:

Bachelor of Arts in English, *summa cum laude*

"Etc."

Avoid "etc." in cover letters—don't expect a potential employer to imagine what else you mean. Either describe it or leave it out.

Serial Comma

Standard editorial practice in a series of items is to use a comma after each item except the last:

Examples: Wynken, Blynken, and Nod
honor, courage, or fame

Slash

Avoid using a slash in place of "and" or "or"; it makes for difficult reading.

Avoid: "Planned/designed/ implemented recreational program. Evaluated/monitored new students' progress. Coached/choreographed performances. Set team goals/incentives to maximize performance."

Content

Ockham's Razor

Ockham's (or Occam's) Razor refers to a saying by a Franciscan monk, William of Ockham (c. 1285–c. 1349): "Pluralitas non est ponenda sine necessitate," or "Entities should not be multiplied unnecessarily." This is usually applied to scientific theories, meaning that the simplest explanation is best (i.e., using the "razor" to cut away whatever is unnecessary to explain a phenomenon). In writing, the idea finds application in using the fewest words and the least punctuation and capitalization necessary to convey the message. More is superfluous.

This idea is the basis for the famous Rule 13 in Strunk and White's *Elements of Style:* "Omit needless words." (In recent printings, Rule 13 has inexplicably been changed to Rule 22, but it's still known to generations of students and writers—and presumably will continue to be known—as Rule 13.)

It says, "A sentence should contain no unnecessary words, a paragraph no unnecessary sentences, for the same reason that a drawing should have no unnecessary lines and a machine no unnecessary parts." This is one way writers achieve power and elegance.

Here are some examples of how Rule 13 would be applied to typical resume language.

Original	Revision
Assisted in preparation of	Assisted in preparing
Responsible for directing	Directed
Performed problem analysis and resolution activities via the company's help line.	Analyzed and resolved problems via the help desk.
Functions I performed included formatting and producing complex documents.	I formatted and produced complex documents.

Tone

A cover letter should steer a middle course between extremely formal, which can come across as pretentious, and extremely informal, which can come across as presumptuous. Try to sound genuine, not stilted. When in doubt, err on the side of formality. Here are some traps to avoid:

Don't give your life story: *Six years ago, I started a career in nursing. I subsequently left to enter business and later opted to resign from a lucrative position to pursue my first career, nursing.*

Don't congratulate them: *I am currently seeking an entry-level opportunity in a successful marketing department and have learned about Any Corporation through the L.A. Top Sellers Guide. Congratulations on such an outstanding year!* It's unlikely they care about your congratulations, which come across as presumptuous and ingratiating. Also, it's evident you wouldn't bother to mention it unless you were looking for a job.

Don't compliment them: *My interest in joining your dynamic staff in a full-time management position has prompted me to forward the enclosed resume for your consideration.*

Don't presume to tell them how useful you'll be or that "we have good reason to meet." Give them credit for knowing what they want: *I am confident that I am the person you seek in your advertisement in the April 15 edition of the* Providence Evening Bulletin.

If you are in need of a highly motivated achiever skilled in selling products and services and developing client relationships and new business, then we have good reason to meet.

As a member of your staff, I would offer . . .

Don't tell them in the cover letter that you want more information: *I recently read your advertisement in the* Boston Globe *for the position of assistant editor and am highly interested in learning more about the job's specific requirements.* If they call, then you can ask.

Don't tell them why you're leaving your current job: *I am currently seeking a career opportunity offering a new scope of responsibility and more permanent challenge requiring creative skills as well as follow-through capability as an individual or member of a production team.* If they're interested in you, they won't care why you're leaving (assuming your record is satisfactory). If they call you and want to know, you can tell them on the phone or at the interview. Mention it in the letter only if it's unavoidable.

Don't philosophize: *Finding the right person for the job is often difficult, costly, and at times disappointing. However, if one of your clients is in need of a reliable, competent, and well-organized individual for their office management staff, I have the qualifications and dedication for the position.*

Don't be grandiose: *As a recent graduate of Tufts University Environmental Leadership Training Program and a 1993 graduate of Mesa State College with a degree in Biology, I am currently launching my career as an environmental campaigner in areas of concern that affect local, national, or world communities.*

Don't be longwinded: *Please accept the enclosed resume as an expressed interest in contributing relevant experience to the position of Sales Representative, as advertised in the* Pittsburgh Post-Gazette, *on Wednesday, April 11.*

Instead: *I would like to apply for the position of sales representative advertised in the* Pittsburgh Post-Gazette.

Currently, as an elementary school teacher responsible for thirty second-grade students, I am actively involved in the development and implementation of reading, writing, and math programs which effectively motivate accomplishment through both individual and group projects.

Find a Computer

If you don't have access to a computer that can be used for job-hunting purposes, fear not! Places such as Kinko's Copies are open twenty-four hours and let you sign in to use a computer for about $12 per hour. This can be well worth the cost if you're typing up a quick cover letter, for example. However, if you're planning on spending a significant amount of time on the computer, you may opt to sign up to use a computer at a public library. Many libraries have a number of computers set aside for public use (including some that have Internet access). Call ahead of time to find out the library's policies.

See also "Ockham's Razor" and "That and Which."

Don't try to make your job sound important: *In my present position, I have gained valuable experience and training in important organizational and operational areas of a company's general business operation.*
Instead: *In my present position, I have gained experience in organization and operations.*

Don't gush—don't use expressions like *I'd be thrilled to . . .* or *I'd love to. . . .*

Don't state the obvious: *I enclose a copy of my resume for your perusal.*

The enclosed resume is a brief summary of my academic accomplishments and work experience. What else would it be?

Don't be fawning or ingratiating: *I am writing with the hope that you will consider me for the position of translator as advertised in today's* Rocky Mountain News. Certainly they'll consider you—that's why they advertised.

I am well organized, detail-oriented, and committed to servicing your corporation in an efficient and productive way. I am very eager to learn more about the responsibilities of the position and how I can begin to make a contribution to your overall success.

I am available any time to learn more about Any Corporation and convince you of my desire to join your ranks.

I look forward to discussing my background and experience in detail with you and would be glad to make myself available for an interview at your convenience.

I currently have a flexible schedule and am available for an interview at almost any time, given advance notice.

I am most anxious to become a part of your firm.

I would appreciate the opportunity to discuss this position with you at your convenience, as it sounds like an exciting opportunity. If you have any questions, do not hesitate to contact me at the above-listed phone number or at (601) 444-4444.

Don't tell them what you want them to do or that you'll call to schedule an interview. Give them credit for being able to figure out what to do if they're interested: *After you have had the opportunity to review my qualifications, I would appreciate hearing from you to schedule a personal interview. I would like to learn more about your needs and discuss my ability to contribute to your goals.*

After you have had the chance to review my resume, please contact me so that we can further discuss the possibility of my joining your staff.

Enclosed is my resume. I would very much like to schedule a mutually convenient interview time. I can be reached at the above address or by phone at (904) 555-5555. The opportunity to join your management team is of great interest to me, and I look forward to meeting with you for further discussion.

Don't tell them to call you—for additional information or any other reason:
If my qualifications interest you, please do not hesitate to contact me. I will be glad to furnish any additional information you require.

Don't repeat the addressee's name in the body of the letter. It comes across as phony and ingratiating: *Thank you, Mr. Cummings, for your help.*

Don't use euphemisms:

A Clear Direction

Employers like job candidates who have real interests and a clear direction. They know that if you're interested in a particular industry, company, or job, you're more likely to enjoy the position, perform well, and stay with the company.

Employers *don't* like to hear that you aren't at all discriminating—that you'll take whatever job they have available.

Instead of	Use
association	position
possess	have
utilize	use *or* apply
in addition	also
as well as	and

Grammar

Can and May

What's wrong with this sentence?

I may be reached at (505) 555-5555 (days) and (505) 444-4444 (evenings).

If you *may* be reached there, why would they waste their time calling? Only if they know you *can* be reached there are they likely to call. But if your number already appears in your letterhead or inside address, which it should, why repeat it?

Fused Participle

I appreciate you taking the time to speak to me is an example of a *fused participle* and is grammatically incorrect. Here, *you* modifies the gerund *taking* and should be an adjective: *I appreciate **your** taking the time to speak to me.*

Sentence Structure

What's wrong with these sentences?

Please accept the enclosed resume for the executive director position at Any Center as advertised in the Los Angeles Times.

Enclosed is my resume, which I submit as a candidate for the hotel manager position as advertised in the Detroit Free Press *on January 23.*

A resume is unlikely to be hired as either an executive director or hotel manager. You are the candidate, not your resume.

That and Which

What's wrong with this sentence?

In my last position which involved responsibility for developing and implementing occupational health programs, I supervised twelve people.

The problem is that the meaning is unclear. Is it this?

In my last position that involved responsibility for developing and implementing occupational health programs, I supervised twelve people. Here, the implication is that the candidate has held more than one such position and is referring to the last one.

Or this?

In my last position, which involved responsibility for developing and implementing occupational health programs, I supervised twelve people. Here, no inference can be drawn about other positions; the candidate is merely providing additional information about the last position.

That introduces a *restrictive* clause—the clause *restricts* the meaning of the preceding clause to a specific set of circumstances. It is essential information and cannot be omitted without changing the meaning of the sentence.

Which preceded by a comma introduces a *nonrestrictive* clause—the clause does not restrict the meaning of the preceding clause. It is merely additional information and can be omitted without changing the meaning of the sentence.

Now it should be clear what's wrong with these sentences:

I have twenty-one years of experience in positions which involved autonomous responsibility for developing and implementing occupational health programs.

I am looking for a new association with an international service-oriented organization which can benefit from my multilingual and organizational skills in a marketing position.

While accomplishing this objective, I developed training procedures which allowed for cross-training, multiethnic, multicultural, production personnel to work at ten assembly stations.

My interest is in joining a firm which has a need for a representative capable of working effectively with clients in real estate development, property management, and finance.

In each case, *which* is being used incorrectly to introduce a restrictive clause.

Instead:

I have twenty-one years of experience in positions that *involved autonomous responsibility for developing and implementing occupational health programs.*

I am looking for a new association with an international service-oriented organization that *can benefit from my multilingual and organizational skills in a marketing position.*

While accomplishing this objective, I developed training procedures that *allowed for cross-training, multiethnic, multicultural, production personnel to work at ten assembly stations.*

My interest is in joining a firm that *has a need for a representative capable of working effectively with clients in real estate development, property management, and finance.*

The correct use of *which* to introduce a nonrestrictive clause requires a comma:

I am aware of Any Corporation's innovative approach to TQM, which has been used as an example across the country.

The determining factor is whether the information in the clause is essential or merely additional. If it's essential, it's preceded by *that* and no comma; if it's additional, it's preceded by a comma and *which.*

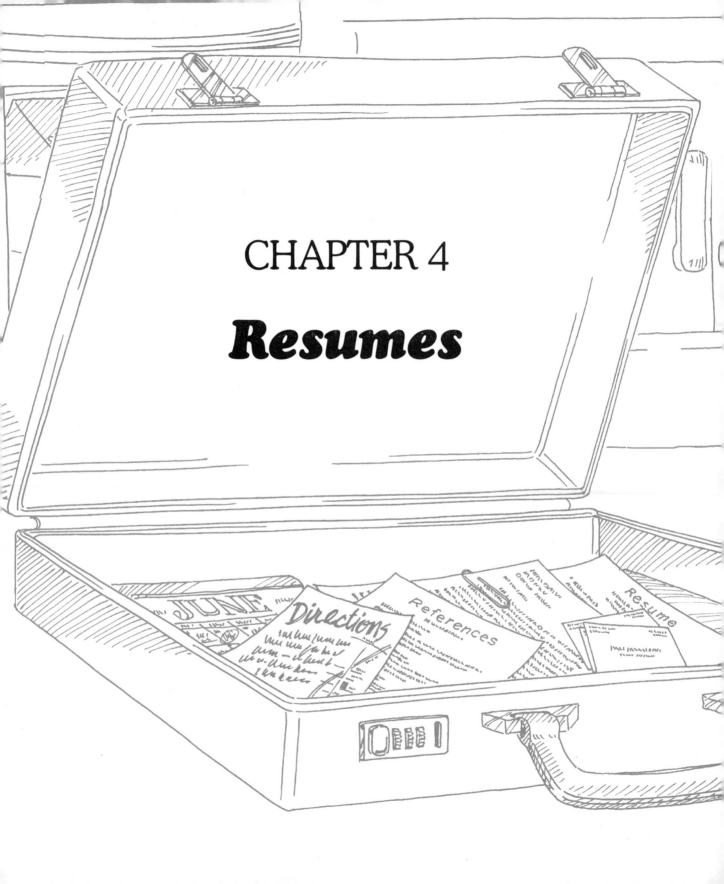

CHAPTER 4

Resumes

Does Your Resume Have an Accent?

Only if you want it to. All three ways are acceptable:

resume
resumé
résumé

When filling a position, an employer will often have a hundred-plus applicants but time to interview only a handful of the most promising ones. As a result, a recruiter will reject most applicants after only briefly skimming their resumes.

Unless you've phoned and talked to the employer—which you should do whenever you can—you'll be chosen or rejected entirely on the basis of your resume and cover letter. *Your cover letter must catch the employer's attention, and your resume must hold it.* (But remember—a resume is no substitute for a job-search campaign. *You* must seek a job. Your resume is only one tool, albeit a critical one.)

Both the appearance, or format, of your resume and the content are important. These are discussed in separate sections below.

Format

First impressions matter, so make sure the recruiter's first impression of your resume is a good one.

Types

The most common resume formats are the chronological resume and the functional resume. You may also see references to a "chrono-functional," or "combination," resume, but this is usually a variant on one of the other two—a chronological type with an expanded skills summary or a functional type with an expanded work-history section.

Chronological

The chronological format is the most common. Choose a chronological format if you're currently working or were working recently and if your most recent experiences relate to your desired field. Use reverse chronological order and include dates. To a recruiter, your last job and your latest schooling are the most important, so put the last first and list the rest going back in time. Remember: There is no need to capitalize "present" in "1999–present."

Functional

A functional resume focuses on skills and strengths that your most recent jobs don't necessarily reflect, while de-emphasizing job titles, employers, etc. A functional resume may be useful if you have no work experience, have been out of the work force for a long time, or are changing careers. But some recruiters may wonder if you're trying to hide something, so be ready for questions of that nature. In some cases, a skills summary section at the top of a chronological resume may be useful.

Typing

A word processing or desktop publishing program is the most common way to generate your resume. This allows you the flexibility to make changes instantly and store different drafts. These programs also offer many different fonts, each taking up different amounts of space. (It's best to stay between 10-point and 12-point type size.) Many other options are also available, like boldface or italics for emphasis and the ability to manipulate spacing. Leave the right-hand margin unjustified to keep the spacing between the letters even and easier to read.

Organization

Your name, phone number, e-mail address (if you have one), and mailing address should be at the top of the resume. Make your name stand out by using a slightly larger font size and boldface. Be sure to spell out everything—don't abbreviate "St." for "Street" or "Rd." for "Road." The word "present" (as in "1997–present") should be lowercase.

Next, list your experience, then your education. If you're a recent graduate, list your education first, unless your experience is more important than your education. (For example, if you've just graduated from a teaching school, have some business experience, and are applying for a job in business, list your business experience first.)

Typeface

Typefaces come in two general categories: *serif* and *sans serif*.

This is a serif face.
This is a sans serif face.

Serif faces are generally easier to read—the serifs and variable thicknesses of the strokes help the eye perceive the letters. They also tend to convey a more upscale image than sans serif. This doesn't mean choosing a fancy, designer typeface—something standard and conservative is best.

Paper Size

Use standard 8½- by 11-inch paper. A smaller size will appear more personal than professional and is easily lost in an employer's files; a larger size will look awkward and may be discarded for not fitting with other documents.

The important thing is to break up the text in some logical way that makes your resume visually attractive and easy to scan, so experiment to see which layout works best. However you set it up, *stay consistent*. Inconsistencies in fonts, spacing, or tenses make your resume look sloppy. Use tabs rather than the less precise space bar to keep information aligned vertically.

Abbreviations

It's advisable to spell out most abbreviations on a resume. Resumes are compressed enough as it its; frequent abbreviations and acronyms can make them nearly unintelligible.

Length

Employers dislike long resumes, so keep it to one page if possible. If you must squeeze in more information than would otherwise fit, try using a slightly smaller typeface or changing the margins. Watch also for "widows" (a word or two on a separate line at the end of a paragraph). You can often free up some space if you can edit the information enough to get rid of those single words taking up an entire line. Another tactic that works with some word processing programs is to decrease the size of your paragraph returns and change the spacing between lines.

Paper Color and Quality

Use quality paper that is standard 8½ by 11 inches and has weight and texture, in a conservative color like white or ivory. Good resume paper is easy to find at stores that sell stationery or office products and is even available at some drugstores. Use *matching* paper and envelopes for both your resume and cover letter. One hiring manager at a major magazine throws out all resumes that arrive on paper that differs in color from the envelope!

Do not buy paper with images of clouds and rainbows in the background or anything that looks like casual stationery you would send your favorite aunt. Do not spray perfume or cologne on your resume. Also, never use the stationery of your current employer.

Printing

For a resume on paper, the result will depend on the quality of the printer you use. Laser printers are best. Do not use a dot matrix printer. If you don't print out each copy individually, use a high-quality photocopier, such as in a professional copy shop.

Household typewriters and office typewriters with nylon or other cloth ribbons are *not* good enough for typing your resume. If you don't have access to a quality word processing program, hire a professional with the resources to prepare your resume for you. Keep in mind that businesses like Kinko's (open twenty-four hours) provide access to computers with quality printers.

Many companies now use scanning equipment to screen the resumes they receive, and certain paper, fonts, and other features are more compatible with this technology. Formatting a resume for scanning is discussed in Chapter 5 **[Electronic Resumes]**.

Watermark

When you print your resume (and cover letter), hold it up to a light to make sure the watermark reads correctly—that it's not upside down or backward. As trivial as this may sound, it's the accepted style in formal correspondence, and some recruiters check for it. One recruiter at a law firm in New Hampshire sheepishly admitted this is the first thing he checks: "I open each envelope and check the watermarks on the resume and cover letter. Those candidates that have it wrong go into a different pile."

Proof with Care

Mistakes on resumes are not only embarrassing, they will often remove you from consideration (particularly if something obvious, like your name, is misspelled). No matter how much you paid someone else to type, write, or typeset your resume, *you* lose if there is a mistake. So proofread it as carefully as possible. Get a friend to help you. Read your draft aloud as your friend checks the proof copy. Then have your friend read aloud while you check. Next, read it letter by letter to check spelling and punctuation.

If you're having it typed or typeset by a resume service or a printer and you don't have time to proof it, pay for it and take it home. Proof it there and bring it back later to get it corrected and printed.

If you wrote your resume with a word processing program, use the built-in spell checker to double-check for spelling errors. Keep in mind that a spell checker will not find errors like "to" for "two" or "wok" for "work." Many spell-check programs don't recognize missing or misused punctuation, nor are they set to check the spelling of capitalized words. It's important to still proofread your resume for grammatical mistakes and other problems, even after it's been spell-checked.

If you find mistakes, do not fix them with pen, pencil, or white-out! Make the changes on the computer and print out the resume again.

Content

Sell Yourself . . .

You're selling your skills and accomplishments in your resume, so it's important to take inventory and know yourself. If you've achieved something, say so. Put it in the best possible light. But avoid subjective statements, like "I am a hard worker" or "I get along well with my coworkers." Stick to the facts.

While you shouldn't hold back or be modest, don't exaggerate your achievements to the point of misrepresentation. Be honest. Many companies will immediately drop an applicant from consideration (or fire a current employee) upon discovering inaccurate or untrue information on a resume or other application material.

. . . But Be Concise

Write down the important (and pertinent) things you've done, but do it in as few words as possible. Short, concise phrases are more effective than long-winded sentences. Avoid the use of "I" when emphasizing your accomplishments. Instead, use phrases beginning with action verbs. Use present tense for your current job and past tense for previous jobs.

Also, try to hold your paragraphs to six lines or fewer. If you have more than six lines of information about one job or school, put it in two or more paragraphs. A short resume will be examined more carefully. Remember: your resume usually has between eight and forty-five seconds to catch an employer's eye, so make every second count.

Give 'Em What They Want

Employers favor certain skills. Here are the top contenders:

- *Supervising/managing skills* mean you can take responsibility for the work of others.
- *Coordinating/organizing skills* allow you to plan events or see projects to completion.
- *Negotiating skills* allow you to bring about compromise and resolve differences.
- *Customer service/public relations skills* enable you to be a spokesperson for your organization.
- *Training/instructing skills* allow you to show newcomers the ropes.
- *Interviewing skills* enable you to ask tough questions, then listen to get insight from the answers.
- *Speaking skills* involve presenting your ideas verbally in a coherent fashion.
- *Writing skills* enable you to express your ideas convincingly on paper.
- *Deadline-meeting skills* enable you to work under pressure.
- *Budgeting skills* involve the ability to save your employer money.

Avoid Catch Phrases

In the course of a job search, it's tempting to use catch phrases you've picked up from advertisements or reference materials, phrases that sound as though they *should* go in a resume or cover letter. Many people are tempted to reach for expressions like "self-starter," "excellent interpersonal skills," and "work well independently or as part of a team."

The Kitchen-Sink Sentence

Being concise doesn't mean trying to cram every facet of your job into a single sentence. Break up long, unwieldy sentences:

Example (wrong way): "Responsible for editing, writing, and production coordination of bid proposals for government, industrial, and utility engineering and construction contracts."

Example (right way): "Prepare bid proposals for government, industrial, and utility contracts, including engineering and construction. Write and edit proposals; coordinate production."

Remember that seemingly efficient strings of nouns can become hard to understand and are often better off broken up for purposes of grammar AND common sense.

The Appropriate Apostrophe

A common mistake on resumes, especially in describing your work experience, is to refer to " . . . over five years experience in. . . ."

"Years" here is a type of possessive and must have an apostrophe: ". . . over five years' experience in. . . ."

Improve on these descriptions by listing actual projects and goals. For example, rephrase "Determined achiever with proven leadership skills" as follows: "Supervised staff of fifteen and increased the number of projects completed before deadline by X percent." Once you begin working, employers will discover your personal attributes for themselves. While you're under consideration, concrete experiences are more valuable than vague phrases or obscure promises.

Job Objective

Objectives tend to sound generic, and the information they contain should be clear from your cover letter. Also, an overly specific objective may eliminate you from consideration for other positions that a recruiter feels are a better match for your qualifications.

In certain instances, an objective may be suitable—for example, if your previous work experience is unrelated to the position for which you're applying, or if you're a recent graduate with no work experience. Sometimes an objective can give a functional resume focus. One or two sentences describing the job you're seeking may clarify the capacity in which your skills can best be put to use. Be sure your objective is in line with the position for which you're applying, and don't state that you're looking for a position that will allow you to grow or to develop certain capacities. Employers are interested in what you can do for them, not what they can do for you. This is something to keep in mind throughout the job-search and interview process.

Experience

Emphasize continued experience in a particular job area or continued interest in a particular industry. De-emphasize irrelevant positions. Delete positions you held for less than four months (unless you're a recent college graduate or still in school). It's okay to include one opening line providing a general description of each company at which you've worked.

Stress your results and achievements, elaborating on how you contributed in your previous jobs. Did you increase sales, reduce costs, improve a product, implement a new program? Were you promoted? Use specific numbers (quantities, percentages, dollar amounts) whenever possible. Always avoid "etc." when presenting

your experiences. Don't expect a potential employer to imagine what else you mean.

Gaps in Your Employment History

You may be asked about gaps in your employment history. Although you'll need to be prepared to explain them, gaps aren't the stigma they used to be. Many people now have some kind of irregularity in their work histories—they were laid off, went back to school, took off for personal reasons, changed careers, had a baby—you name it. Because this is now so prevalent, recruiters can't very well hold it against you, as long as you have a plausible explanation and the skills for the job.

Action Verbs

In describing previous work experiences, the strongest resumes use short phrases beginning with action verbs. Remember, however, that if you upload your resume to an on-line job hunting site like CareerCity, the keywords or key nouns a computer would search for become as important as action verbs. For more on keywords in electronic resumes, see Chapter 5 **[Electronic Resumes]**.

Bullets

Bullets are useful for drawing attention to significant points, but make sure that your resume is not too bullety. A long column of bullet points in random order can lack cohesion. An alternative is to group them conceptually—in relevant categories, with a few bullets under each one—to make them easier to grasp. This may also permit you to combine several bullets into one or, conversely, to break up long paragraphs. Do remember, however, that bulleted blocks, capitals, or italics are hard to read and are best avoided. Also, periods following elements of bulleted lists are optional. The general rule is to use periods for statements that are full sentences; otherwise don't.

Avoid Excessive Jargon and Excessive Words

Some technical terms may be necessary, but try to avoid excessive "technicalese." Keep in mind that the first person to see your resume may be a human resources person, who won't necessarily know all the jargon—and can't be impressed by something he or

Volunteer Work

If you would like to include your volunteer work with your paid work experiences to give your resume a more continuous work history, make sure to title this section "Experience" rather than "Employment Background" or "Professional Experience."

The Third Degree on Your "Degree"

Cum laude, magna cum laude, and *summa cum laude* are lowercase and italic:

Bachelor of Arts in English, *summa cum laude*

"B.A. degree in . . ." is redundant. Just "B.A. in . . ." is fine. Also, don't say "Associates degree in . . ." or "Masters in. . . ." You may have an associate's degree or a master's degree (with apostrophes), but on a resume you would say "Associate in [or "of"] Arts" or "Master of Arts."

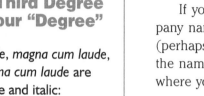

she doesn't understand. Also strive to use the fewest number necessary to convey your message. Example: "Responsible for directing" can be "Directed" (if a past experience) or "Direct" (if current).

Temporary Work

If you do your temporary work through an agency, list the company name and job description for any longer-term assignments (perhaps a month or longer) you held. For shorter assignments, use the name of the agency, but also list the names of companies where you worked.

ProTemps Employment, Houston, TX

Short-term clerk/typist assignments at the following companies:
Acme Products
Bonding Devices
Development Partners
Morrison Manufacturing
Terragard Fabrics

Skills

Most jobs now require computer knowledge. Therefore, it's usually advisable to include a section titled "Computer Skills," in which you list software programs you know. If the list is long, subdivide them by category.

Example:	
Operating systems	DOS, Windows, Macintosh
Writing/publishing tools	Word, WordPerfect, QuarkXPress, PageMaker, Photoshop, Illustrator
Business [or *Financial*]	Excel, Lotus 1-2-3, Access
Languages	C++, BASIC

It isn't usually necessary to include the version number of an application. Nor do you need to be perfectly fluent with a program to list it. As long as you've used it in the past and could pick it up again with a little practice, it's legitimate to include it.

The skills section is also an ideal place to mention fluency in a foreign language. If you're listing skills other than computer knowledge, subdivide them by category under the "Skills" heading: "Computer," "Languages," etc.

Education

Keep the education section brief if you have more than two years of career experience. Elaborate more if you have less experience. If you're a recent college graduate, you may choose to include high school activities that are *directly* relevant to your career.

Mention degrees received and any honors or special awards. Note individual courses that might be relevant to employers. (These should be at least a semester long. Shorter courses of a day or two, even a week or two, should not generally be mentioned unless they're important in your field. It's also unnecessary to list courses taken in pursuit of a degree.)

Certifications

Mention any applicable certifications or licenses you hold, such as teaching or social work.

Personal Information

Do not include your age, health, physical characteristics, marital status, race, religion, political/moral beliefs, or any other personal information. List your personal interests and hobbies only if they're directly relevant to the type of job you're seeking. If you're applying to a company that greatly values teamwork, for instance, citing that you organized a community fundraiser or played on a basketball team may be advantageous. When in doubt, however, leave it out.

Do not include your picture with your resume unless you have a specific and appropriate reason to do so—for example, if you're applying for a job as an actor or model.

Professional Affiliations

These are worth noting if you're a member of a professional organization in your industry.

It's Illegal

"Those things [marital status, church affiliations, etc.] have no place on a resume. Those are illegal questions, so why even put that information on your resume?"

—BECKY HAYES
CAREER COUNSELOR,
CAREER SERVICES,
RICE UNIVERSITY

References

"References available upon request" is unnecessary on a resume. It's understood that if you're considered for the position, you'll be asked for references and will provide them. Don't send references with your resume and cover letter unless they're specifically requested.

When to Get Help

If you write reasonably well, it's to your advantage to write your own resume. This forces you to review your experiences and figure out how to explain your accomplishments in clear, brief phrases. This will help you when you explain your work to interviewers. It's also easier to tailor your resume to each position you're applying for when you've put it together yourself.

If you have difficulty writing in resume style (which is quite unlike normal written language), if you're unsure which parts of your background to emphasize, or if you think your resume would make your case better if it didn't follow one of the standard forms outlined either here or in a book on resumes, consider having it professionally written.

The best way to choose a resume writer is by reputation: the recommendation of a friend, a personnel director, your school placement officer, or someone else knowledgeable in the field.

Important questions:
"How long have you been writing resumes?"
"If I'm not satisfied with what you write, will you go over it with me and change it?"
"Do you charge by the hour or a flat rate?"

For more information on resume services, contact the Professional Association of Resume Writers at 3637 Fourth Street, Suite 330, St. Petersburg, FL 33704, USA. Correspondence can be addressed to the attention of Mr. Frank Fox, Executive Director.

Price and Quality

There is no guaranteed relation between price and quality, except that you're unlikely to get a good writer for less than $50 for an uncomplicated resume, and you shouldn't have to pay more than $300 unless your experience is extensive or complicated. Printing charges will be extra. Assume nothing, no matter how much you pay. It's your career at stake if your resume has mistakes!

Few resume services will give you a firm price over the phone, simply because some resumes are too complicated and take too long to do for a predetermined price. Some services will quote you a price that applies to almost all of their customers. Once you decide to use a specific writer, you should insist on a firm price quote *before* engaging his or her services. Also, find out how expensive minor changes will be.

For Students and Recent Graduates

Which Type of Resume Is Right for You?

The type of resume you use depends on your job experience. If you don't have any work history, use a functional resume format, emphasizing your strong points:

Education. This should be your primary focus.
Special achievements. This could be almost anything from having an article published to graduating with honors.
Awards and competitive scholarships
Classes, internships, theses, or special projects that relate to your job objective
Computer knowledge. Are you familiar with a Mac or PC? What software programs do you know?
Language skills. Are you fluent in a foreign language? Be sure to indicate both written and verbal skills.
Volunteer work
Committees and organizations
Extracurricular activities

Show It to People

"The one piece of advice I give to everyone about their resume is: Show it to people, show it to people, show it to people. Before you ever send out a resume, show it to at least a dozen people."

—Cate Talbot Ashton
Associate Director,
Career Services,
Colby College

The Punctuation Situation

Serial Comma
Standard editorial practice in a series of items is to use a comma after each item except the last item:
" . . . server, lifeguard, and courier."

Colons and Subheads
It's generally unnecessary to use a colon after a subhead. The function of the subhead is to set off and describe what follows; the colon is unnecessary. Rarely are more than three levels of subheads necessary.

Recruiters like to see some kind of work history, even if it doesn't relate to your job objective, because it demonstrates that you have a good work ethic. However, it's also important to emphasize special skills or qualifications, including the above information.

Work History

When describing your work history, avoid simply listing your job duties. Focus on accomplishments and achievements, even if they're small. Consider the difference:

Weak: "Lifeguard at busy public beach. Responsible for safety of bathers and cleanliness of the beach and parking areas."

Strong: "Lifeguard at busy public beach. Rescued eight people during summer. Established recycling program for bottles and cans."

If you've held many jobs, you may choose to emphasize only two or three of the most relevant and list the rest under the heading "Other Experience" without individual job descriptions:

Other Experience: Floor and stockroom clerk at university bookstore, server, lifeguard, and courier.

When Functional Is Appropriate

As indicated earlier, under some circumstances, a functional resume may be more appropriate. These may include the following:

- You haven't worked for over a year.
- You want to highlight specific skills by category that would not stand out as easily with a chronological format.
- You've held a variety of jobs.
- Your career goal has taken a dramatic turn.

In this case, a functional resume may be more suitable. It focuses not so much on what positions you've held and when but on what you've learned from your experiences that would be of use in the job.

In certain fields, it is requested that you send a Curriculum Vitae, or "CV," instead of a resume. Sometimes this is referred to as an "International Resume," since all European countries use some form of the Vitae. A CV is mainly used when applying for jobs in the education and health-care industries.

A CV differs from a resume in that it is tailored toward these industries by providing specific, more comprehensive information. It is usually longer in length, depending on the applicant's degree of experience. Typically, a CV is anywhere from two to eight pages (with those who have a master's degree or more experience at the higher end of the scale). A CV contains information such as:

- Details on educational background including degrees and certificates accrued, master's thesis and/or doctoral dissertation, honors and awards, and GPA.

- A summary of relevant work experience.

- A list of publications authored.

- A list of papers presented at conferences.

- Professional association membership(s).

The functions you served in your old jobs are the crux of this format. The actual titles and dates don't come until the very end.

GPA

Never include a grade point average (GPA) under 3.0 on your resume. If your GPA in your major is higher than your overall GPA, include it either in addition to or instead of your overall GPA.

High School Information

Including high school information is optional for college graduates, but such information should be used sparingly. If you have exceptional achievements in college and in summer or part-time jobs, omit your high school information. High school information should really only be used if the experience is directly related to the types of jobs or industry for which you are applying. If you decide to include high school achievements, describe them more briefly than your college achievements.

Keep in Touch

Put your home address and phone number at the top of the resume. Change the message on your answering machine if necessary—the Beastie Boys blaring in the background or your sorority sisters screaming may not come across well to all recruiters. If you think you may be moving within six months, include a second address and phone number of a trusted friend or relative who can reach you no matter where you are.

Remember that employers may keep your resume on file and contact you months later if a position opens that fits your qualifications. All too often, candidates are unreachable because they moved and didn't provide enough contact options on their resumes.

CHAPTER 5

Electronic Resumes

Many companies use automated applicant tracking systems to process and sort employment applications. Others use the services of electronic employment database companies to fill specific openings. This means that your resume will be read by more computers and fewer people. Whether you're applying to a company that uses automated tracking systems or paying to have your resume loaded onto an electronic employment database or on-line database, your resume must be in a format that's easy for a computer to recognize. Otherwise, your application may quickly begin collecting dust.

The good news about this technology is that it enables you to market your resume to thousands of employers quite easily. The bad news is that you must create an electronic resume in order to take advantage of the technology. An electronic resume is simply a modified version of your conventional resume.

Before you go ahead and throw out your old paper resume, be advised that not all companies stay up to speed on the latest technology. Many companies simply don't have the equipment to directly receive e-mailed resumes and search on-line databases for job candidates. Having a paper copy of your resume is still a necessity, especially since you'll need it to bring with you to all those job interviews!

Format

Keep your resume simple. The same elaborate formatting that makes your resume beautiful for the human eye to behold makes it impossible for a computer to understand.

Length

Your resume should be no longer than one page, except in unusual circumstances.

Abbreviations

Most resume scanning systems recognize a few common abbreviations, like BS, MBA, and state names, with or without periods.

Widely used acronyms for industry jargon, like A/R and A/P on an accounting resume, are also generally accepted, although it's advisable to spell out most abbreviations. If there's any question about whether an abbreviation is standard, play it safe and spell it out.

Paper

Don't bother with expensive paper. Use standard, twenty-pound, 8½- by 11-inch paper. Because your resume needs to be as sharp and legible as possible, your best bet is to use black ink on white paper.

Font

Stick to the basics; this is no time to express your creativity. Choose a nondecorative font with clear, distinct characters, like Times or Helvetica. It's more difficult for a scanner to accurately pick up decorative fonts like script. Usually the results are unintelligible letters and words.

Size

A size of 12 points is ideal. Don't go below 10 points, as type that's too small may not scan well.

Style

Most scanners will accept boldface, but if a potential employer specifically tells you to avoid it, you can substitute all capital letters. Boldface and capitals are best used only for major section headings, like "Experience" and "Education." Avoid boldface for your name, address, and telephone number. It's also best to avoid italics or underlining, since this can make the words unintelligible.

Graphics, Lines, and Shading

Avoid the temptation to use lines and graphics to liven up what is an otherwise visually uninteresting resume. A resume scanner will try to "read" graphics, lines, and shading as text, resulting in computer chaos. Also avoid nontraditional layouts, like two-column formats.

Should You Include a Cover Letter with Your Electronic Resume?

Yes. While your cover letter won't help in the initial selection process, it can distinguish you from the competition in the final rounds. If you've taken the time to craft a letter that summarizes your strongest qualifications, you'll have the edge over other contenders who skip this important step.

If you're responding to a classified ad, try to use some of the same keywords the ad mentions. And if you're sending your resume to a new networking contact, be sure to mention who referred you. Even in this anonymous electronic age, the old adage "It's not what you know but who you know" still holds true.

White Space

Don't try to compress space between letters, words, or lines to fit everything on one page—this makes it more difficult for the computer to read. Leave plenty of space between sections.

Printing

Make sure the result is letter quality. Avoid typewriters and dot matrix printers, since the quality of type they produce is inadequate for most scanners. Because your resume needs to be as sharp and legible as possible, always send an original, not a photocopy, and mail your resume rather than faxing it. For the same reason, in the unlikely event your resume is longer than one page, don't staple the pages together.

Content

The information you include in your electronic resume doesn't really differ from a traditional resume—it's simply the manner in which you present it that changes. Traditionally, resumes include action verbs, like "managed," "coordinated," or "developed." Now, employers are more likely to do keyword searches filled with nouns, like degree held or software you're familiar with. Personal traits are rarely used in keyword searches by employers, but when they are, traits like team player, creative, and problem-solving are among the most common.

Keywords

Using the right keywords or key phrases in your resume is critical. Keyword searches tend to focus on nouns. Let's say an employer searches an employment database for a sales representative with the following keyword criteria: sales representative, BS/BA, exceeded quota, cold calls, high energy, willing to travel. Even if you have the right qualifications, if you don't use these keywords on your resume, the computer will pass over your application. To complicate matters further, different employers search for different keywords.

These are usually buzzwords common to your field or industry that describe your experience, education, skills, and abilities.

Although there is no way to know for sure which keywords employers are most likely to search for, you can make educated guesses. Check help-wanted advertisements for job openings in your field. What terms do employers commonly use to describe their requirements? Job seekers in your field are another source, as are executive recruiters who specialize in your field. You'll want to use as many keywords in your resume as possible, but keep in mind that using the same keyword five times won't increase your chances of getting matched with an employer. Note, however, that if you're posting your resume to a job hunting Web site, a small number of such sites rank resumes by the number of keywords and their frequency of occurrence. Your best bet is to find out ahead of time by reading the information on the site.

Name

Your name should appear at the top of the resume, with your address, telephone number, and e-mail address immediately underneath.

Keyword Summary

This is a compendium of your qualifications, usually written in a series of succinct keyword phrases that immediately follow your name and address. Place the most important words first on the list, since the computer may be limited in the number of words it will read.

Objective

As with traditional resumes, including a job objective is advisable only in certain circumstances. (See Chapter 4 [**Resumes**].) If you choose to use a job objective, try to keep it general, so as not to limit your opportunities. After all, while the computer does the initial screening, your resume will eventually be seen by a human hiring manager. Your objective should express a general interest in a particular field or industry ("an entry-level position in advertising")

What Is HTML?

HTML (hypertext markup language) is the text formatting language used to publish information on the World Wide Web. With HTML, you can format your resume on the Web the way you did on paper, using different fonts, sizes, boldface, italics, and so on. Otherwise it would appear just as lines of unformatted text.

but should not designate a specific job title ("a position as a senior agency recruitment specialist"). Include a few keywords in the objective, to increase your chances of getting matched ("a position as a financial analyst where I can utilize my on-the-job experience and MBA").

Experience and Achievements

Your professional experience should immediately follow the keyword summary, beginning with your most recent position. (If you're a recent college graduate, list your education before your experience.) Be sure your job title, employer, location, and dates of employment are all clearly displayed. Highlight your accomplishments and key responsibilities with dashes (in place of bullets) on an electronic resume. Again, try to incorporate as many buzzwords as possible into these phrases.

Education

This section immediately follows the experience section. List your degrees, licenses, permits, certifications, relevant course work, and academic awards or honors. Be sure to clearly display the names of the schools, locations, and years of graduation. List any professional organizations or associations you're a member of; many recruiters will include such organizations when doing a keyword search.

References

Don't waste valuable space with statements like "References available upon request." Although this was standard fare for resumes of old, it won't win you any points on an electronic resume.

Personal Data

Don't include personal data, like your birthdate, marital status, or information regarding your hobbies and interests. Since it's unlikely these sections would include any keywords, they're only taking up space, and the computer will pass right over them.

Circulating Your Electronic Resume

Once you've designed a computer-friendly resume, you can circulate it in three ways. The first is to send it to a company with an in-house resume database or applicant tracking system. Whenever there's an opening, the hiring manager submits a search request, which generally includes a job description and a list of keywords. An operator searches the database to come up with viable candidates.

The second way is to send your resume to an electronic employment database service. When outside companies need candidates for a job opening, they contact the service and provide a list of qualifications (or keywords) the position requires. The service then searches the database (using a keyword search) to find suitable candidates.

The third way is to post your resume via the Internet, either by e-mail, to an on-line database service (this is the same as an electronic employment database service, except that you send your resume electronically rather than by mail), a site on the World Wide Web, a commercial on-line service (like America Online or CompuServe), or a newsgroup. Another option is to create a resume in HTML and post it to special sites on the Web that accept HTML resumes. You can even design your own home page for potential employers to visit. (For more information on using the Internet as a job search tool, see Chapter 6.)

An Electronic Resume for Scanning

On page 74 is an example of an electronic resume for scanning containing no bullets, italics, or underlining. All text begins flush left, with spaces between paragraphs and sections. Boldface is usually acceptable, but if not, capital letters may be substituted.

An Electronic Resume for E-mail

On page 75 is the same resume prepared for e-mail. Remember that each line must be **sixty-five characters or less.**

Cover Letters by E-mail

Omit a cover letter only if the ad to which you are responding says to. Send your cover letter in the same e-mail as your resume (preceding it, of course), and be as attentive to your grammar and spelling as with a paper cover letter. Because this way of sending information is so quick, more and more jobseekers are forgetting that the same rules apply. Sloppy cover letters via e-mail will be viewed just as poorly as sloppy work sent by regular mail.

An Electronic Resume for Scanning

Michael S. Dipenstein
27 Pageant Drive, Apartment 7
Cambridge, MA 02138
(617) 555-5555

KEYWORD SUMMARY
Accounting manager with seven years' experience in general ledger, accounts payable, and financial reporting. MBA in Management. Windows, Lotus 1-2-3, and Excel.

PROFESSIONAL EXPERIENCE
COLWELL CORPORATION, Wellesley, MA

Accounting Manager   1996–present

Manage a staff of six in general ledger and accounts payable. Responsible for the design and refinement of financial reporting package. Assist in month-end closings.

Established guidelines for month-end closing procedures, speeding up closing by five business days.

FRANKLIN AND DELANY COMPANY, Melrose, MA

Senior Accountant   1994–96

Managed accounts payable, general ledger, transaction processing, and financial reporting. Supervised staff of two.

Developed management reporting package, including variance reports and cash flow reporting.

Staff Accountant   1993–94

Managed accounts payable, including vouchering, cash disbursements, and bank reconciliation. Wrote and issued policies. Trained new employees.

EDUCATION
MBA in Management, Northeastern University, Boston, MA, 1995
BS in Accounting, Boston College, Boston, MA, 1993

ASSOCIATIONS
National Association of Accountants

An Electronic Resume for E-mail

```
Michael S. Dipenstein
27 Pageant Drive, Apartment 7
Cambridge, MA 02138
(617) 555-5555

KEYWORD SUMMARY
Accounting manager with seven years' experience in general ledger,
accounts payable, and financial reporting. MBA in Management.
Proficient in Windows, Lotus 1-2-3, and Excel.

PROFESSIONAL EXPERIENCE
COLWELL CORPORATION, Wellesley, MA

Accounting Manager                                        1996 - present

Manage a staff of six in general ledger and accounts payable.
Responsible for the design and refinement of financial reporting
package. Assist in month-end closings.

Established guidelines for month-end closing procedures, speeding up
closing by five business days.

FRANKLIN AND DELANY COMPANY, Melrose, MA

Senior Accountant                                              1994 - 96

Managed accounts payable, general ledger, transaction processing, and
financial reporting. Supervised staff of two.

Developed management reporting package, including variance reports and
cash flow reporting.

Staff Accountant                                               1993 - 94

Managed accounts payable, including vouchering, cash disbursements, and
bank reconciliation. Wrote and issued policies. Trained new employees.

EDUCATION
MBA in Management, Northeastern University, Boston, MA, 1995
BS in Accounting, Boston College, Boston, MA, 1993

ASSOCIATIONS
National Association of Accountants
```

Applicant Tracking Systems

As the name implies, applicant tracking systems, or in-house resume databases, are used by companies to keep track of the hordes of resumes they receive. Many companies, especially large, well-known companies, can receive two hundred resumes per week. Where once these unsolicited resumes may have headed straight for a filing cabinet or even the trash, never to be looked at again, electronic applicant tracking systems now allow employers to keep resumes in an active file.

Basically, here's how it works: a company receives your resume, either unsolicited, through a career fair, or in response to a classified advertisement. Your resume is scanned into the computer, dated, coded, and placed into the appropriate file (like administrative, financial, or technical). Other systems may simply sort resumes according to date received.

When there's a job opening, the hiring manager submits a search request to the database operator, who is usually someone in human resources or information systems. The database operator performs a keyword search to find resumes that match the criteria.

Electronic Employment Databases

An electronic employment database is simply an applicant tracking system operated by an independent commercial firm. The procedure for submitting resumes to these services varies, and most charge a nominal fee, usually $30–50. But what you get for your money is fabulous: nationwide exposure to hundreds of companies of all sizes, from Fortune 500 to smaller, rapidly expanding companies.

In many ways, an electronic resume database is similar to a traditional employment agency: you send in your resume to a service, and the service begins working to find a job for you. However, with an electronic employment "agency," you are, theoretically, in the running for every job request that comes in.

Posting Your Resume Via the Internet

To remain truly competitive, your resume needs to be in a plain-text format you can send to employers and on-line databases electronically through cyberspace.

Converting Your Resume to a Plain-Text File

An electronic resume is sparsely formatted but is filled with keywords and important facts. If you've already prepared a resume that's computer-friendly, you don't have far to go to be able to post your resume on the Internet. A plain-text resume is the next step.

Instead of a Microsoft Word, WordPerfect, or other word processing document, save your resume as a plain-text, DOS, or ASCII file. These three terms are basically interchangeable; different software will use different terms. These words describe text at its simplest, most basic level, without formatting like boldface or italics. Furthermore, an ASCII document appears on the recipient's screen as left-aligned. If you have e-mail, your messages are written and received in this format. By converting your resume to a plain-text file, you can be assured it will be readable, regardless of where you send it.

Before you attempt to create your own plain-text resume, study the resumes on the on-line databases. This will give you a good idea of what a plain-text resume looks like and will help you create your own.

Following are the basic steps for creating a plain-text resume. The particulars of the process will differ, depending on what type of computer system and software you're using:

1. Remove all formatting from your resume. This includes boldface, italics, underlining, bullets, different font sizes, lines, and any and all graphics. To highlight certain parts of your resume, like education or experience, you may use capital letters. You can also use hyphens (-) or asterisks (*) to

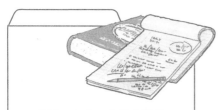

What Is ASCII?

ASCII stands for American Standard Code for Information Interchange and is pronounced "*Ask*-ee." ASCII is a code that virtually all computers can understand. It was invented to allow different types of computers to exchange information easily.

emphasize certain accomplishments or experiences. Leave a blank line or two between sections.

2. Save your resume as a plain-text file. Most word processing programs, like Word and WordPerfect, have a "Save As" feature that allows you to save files in different formats. Some of your options in Word for Windows, for instance, are saving a document as a Word document, a text-only document, or a WordPerfect document. Many programs, like Word, don't specifically give you an "ASCII" option; in these programs, choose "Text Only" or "Plain Text." In Word, plain-text files have the extension ".txt."

3. After saving your resume as a plain-text file, check the document with the text editor that most computers have. In Windows, use Notepad. Open the file to be sure your margins look right and that you don't have extra spaces between lines or letters. If parts of the text are garbled, with a group of strange characters, it most likely means you forgot to take out some formatting. A resume with a lot of formatting is likely to end up looking like hieroglyphics if it's read as a plain-text file. If this happens, go back to your original document and repeat the process.

4. Be sure all the lines contain sixty-five characters or fewer. This includes all spacing, letters, and punctuation. Often you will need to go through your entire resume line by line, counting each space, letter, punctuation, asterisk, and so forth. You may need to manually insert hard returns where the lines are longer than sixty-five characters. This may seem trivial, but it's actually extremely important. While some computers may recognize as many as seventy-five characters per line, the majority cannot recognize more than sixty-five characters.

5. Finally, e-mail your resume to yourself or a friend to test the file. Be sure it stays intact, that no extra spaces or returns are inserted during transmission, and that all text appears readable. If something doesn't look right, go back to your text editor, fix the problem, and test the resume again before e-mailing it to any companies or posting it to on-line databases.

E-mail

E-mailing your resume to potential employers is generally done in response to a help-wanted advertisement or simply as a method of direct contact. In fact, many companies now request that resumes be submitted through e-mail, rather than the U.S. mail or by fax machine. Some job listings that you find on the Internet, particularly for technical positions, include only an e-mail address for contact information; no street address or telephone number is provided. And with many companies, you can e-mail your resume directly into their in-house resume database. This eliminates the concern that it will be found unreadable by a computerized resume scanner. When e-mailing, paste your resume into the body of the message; many companies won't open an attachment because of the possibility that it may contain a computer virus.

After e-mailing your resume, wait a few days to be sure the recipient has read it. Call or e-mail the company to confirm that your resume was received intact. As with a paper resume, an e-mailed resume may do you little good unless you follow up to express your genuine interest. If you sent your resume to an individual, ask if he or she would like you to elaborate on any sections of your resume. If you sent it to a general e-mail address, call the human resources department to check the status of your application.

On-line Resume Databases

On-line resume databases are similar to electronic employment databases. Cyberspace offers three main areas for resume posting: the World Wide Web, commercial on-line services, and Usenet newsgroups. These sites range from the general *www.hotresume.com* to the specific *www.medsearch.com*. Of the three areas, you'll find the most options on the Web. Virtually all the major job-search sites on the Web, like Monster.com and E-Span, offer resume databases. One major database service, the Worldwide Resume/Talent Bank, is accessible through both the Internet and America Online. The Web

Confidentiality

Many job seekers are wary of on-line resume database services because of issues of confidentiality. When your resume is on-line, it's accessible to virtually anyone with a computer and an Internet connection. This includes personal information like your name, address, telephone number, and other details. This lack of control over who sees their resume worries many job seekers. You may receive phone calls or e-mail messages from companies, organizations, and individuals you have absolutely no interest in.

However, the biggest concern to most job seekers is, what if one of those twenty million people cruising the Internet happens to be your boss? Many services offer safeguards to ensure that this doesn't happen.

(continued on next page)

also contains dozens of other sites for resume posting, including the only sites where you can post HTML resumes.

Bulletin Board Systems (BBSs), Gopher, and Telnet aren't generally considered destinations for resume posting and are best used to find job listings or gather information on specific industries and employers. While you may post resumes to most Bulletin Board Systems, they're not an efficient way to circulate your resume. For this reason, you're better off sticking to sites on the Web and Usenet newsgroups.

Major Resume Sites on the Web

Following are just some of the major job-search sites on the Web where you can post your resume. For a more complete list of job-search sites, see Chapter 6 [**Internet Job Search**].

Unlike Usenet newsgroup databases, resume posting sites on the Web typically contain resumes from job seekers everywhere, which means that thousands of employers search the databases for potential candidates. For this reason, it's a good idea to add a line to your resume stating whether you're willing to relocate.

CareerCity *www.careercity.com* is "The Web's Big Career Site" giving job hunters access to tens of thousands of jobs via three search engines: its own CareerCity jobs database; a newsgroup job-search engine covering hundreds of newsgroups; and addresses, phone numbers, descriptions, and hot links to 27,000 major U.S. employers. You'll find access to thousands of executive search firms and employment agencies, comprehensive salary surveys for all fields, and directories of associations and other industry resources. CareerCity's easy-to-use resume database gives job seekers the opportunity to market their qualifications free to employers subscribing to the database. The site is filled with hundreds of articles on getting started, changing careers, job interviews, resumes, cover letters, and more.

CareerMart *www.careermart.com* features its "Resume Bank" which offers free resume postings to job seekers, and its "E-mail Agent" which automatically notifies you when new positions crop up. Run by BSA Advertising, the site offers links to more than four hundred major employers and some seven hundred colleges and universities. Resumes should be submitted as text files.

CareerMosaic *www.careermosaic.com* has a database called ResumeCM, which contains resumes from job seekers in all geographic areas and occupations. Besides the database on the Web, it also indexes the most popular Usenet newsgroups and automatically adds your resume to their databases. Unlike most databases, ResumeCM also allows employers to conduct a full-text search of your resume instead of searching only subject lines.

Career Shop *www.careershop.com* has a site produced by TenKey Interactive which enables you to post your resume and also e-mail it directly to employers, free. Career Shop also offers a jobs database and allows employers who register with them to search the resume database free.

CareerSite *www.careersite.com* is a free service of Virtual Resources Corporation. CareerSite's resume database allows you to submit your resume as a fully formatted document. You simply fill in some fields on-line to summarize your credentials. Information is presented to participating employers without your name and address, and your resume isn't released to a company without your consent—a great relief to job seekers concerned with confidentiality.

E-Span's JobOptions

www.joboptions.com/esp/plsql/espan_enter.espan_home is available to thousands of employers. E-Span's JobOptions Resume Database allows you to enter your resume data into a section that formats the information for you, or you may paste in your resume as a plain text file.

(continued from previous page)

The resume posting site *Monster.com,* for example, hides your personal information from employers until after they've purchased access to your resume. Some allow you to submit names of companies you'd prefer not receive your resume. Others will contact you to get your permission before forwarding your resume or employment profile to a company. Still others allow you to join the database anonymously—that is, your name, company names, education, and other identifying characteristics won't be shown to prospective employers. There are also a number of Web sites that don't offer these safeguards, so you'll want to check with your service to determine its particular policy.

A Word of Caution

Before writing a check or giving your credit card number to a company over the Internet, it's a good idea to check its reputation with the Better Business Bureau or a similar agency. While the majority of companies selling services over the Internet are reputable, remember that simply because a company has a presence on the Internet doesn't mean it's legitimate.

Monster.com *www.monster.com* has its Resume On-Line Database that allows you to paste either plain text or HTML resumes. Monster.com protects applicants by keeping their personal information, including name and address, separated from the resume. Employers can access that information only after they ve purchased the resume.

CHAPTER 6

Internet Job Search

The Internet consists of four separate areas: the World Wide Web, Usenet, Telnet, and Gopher. These areas include hundreds of thousands of job listings. Bulletin Board Systems (BBSs), which represent a part of cyberspace that doesn't fall into these areas, are also an excellent job-search resource. No surprise, then, that when most people think of electronic job searching, they think of the Internet.

The World Wide Web. The Web is the best-known area of the Internet. It has dozens of excellent electronic career centers that offer all kinds of job-search advice and information, including a growing number of large databases of job listings. The Web has by far the largest collection of job listings found on-line.

Usenet. The User's Network is comprised of more than 20,000 newsgroups, or electronic discussion groups, where people can exchange information, discuss ideas, or just chat. The nature of Usenet makes it a natural for networking—with so many different newsgroups to choose from, you're sure to find one in your field of interest. Usenet is also an outstanding resource for job listings, with over 100,000 offerings.

Telnet. Telnet is the smallest area of the Internet, and getting smaller. Telnet is a good place to look for federal job listings and other information regarding applying for a federal job. It's also useful as a way of connecting to other sites, like a Gopher server.

Gopher. Gopher is a menu-based system of organizing information on the Internet. It was also the first step in making the Internet more user-friendly, with its easy-to-manage menus and powerful search engines, Veronica and Jughead. Because it was developed at the University of Minnesota and quickly became a favorite of academics at other universities, Gopher remains a good source of academic and other specialized job listings. For example, it has one of the few on-line employment resources dedicated to the arts. However, Gopher's popularity is fading in competition with the Web and Usenet newsgroups.

The World Wide Web

The Web is fast becoming the place to look for jobs on the Internet. Dozens of career resources on the Web are devoted to job listings, with more springing up every day. Unlike Usenet newsgroups, which tend to focus on computer-related or other technical positions, the Web has listings for job hunters of all backgrounds.

Major Sites

The Web's job databases vary greatly in both the quality and quantity of job listings. Start with the all-purpose job-search sites, like CareerCity, CareerMosaic, Job Options, and the Monster Board. These are four of the largest and most popular job-search sites on the Web.

A number of listings in the major job databases overlap. The same search performed on the Monster Board and CareerSite, for example, will likely retrieve many of the same listings. Keep careful records, so you don't mistakenly send a resume to the same company twice for the same job.

It's Good to Know . . .

An understanding and knowledge of computers is the most sought-after skill in new employees. Using electronic resources to find a job demonstrates your computer savvy to an employer.

Electronic business directories, either on-line or on CD-ROM, allow you to identify companies that hire employees in your field and with your background. These databases also contain enough company information to give you an indication of whether a company is right for you.

The Internet and commercial on-line services are available twenty-four hours a day, and their national and international scope are ideal for job seekers.

JOB HUNTING SITES FOR EVERYONE

ADGUIDE'S COLLEGE RECRUITER EMPLOYMENT
   SITE: *www.adguide.com*
AMERICAN JOBS: *www.americanjobs.com*
BEST JOBS USA: *www.bestjobsusa.com*
BLACKWORLD: *www.blackworld.com/careers.htm*
BUSINESS JOB FINDER:
   www.cob.ohio-state.edu/dept/fin/osujobs.htm
THE CAREERBUILDER NETWORK:
   www.careerbuilder.com
CAREERCITY: *www.careercity.com*
CAREER CONNECTION: *www.connectme.com*
CAREER EXCHANGE: *www.careerexchange.com*
CAREER EXPOSURE: *www.careerexposure.com*
CAREERLINK USA: *www.careerlinkusa.com*
CAREERMAGAZINE: *www.careermag.com*
CAREERMART: *www.careermart.com*
CAREERMOSAIC: *www.careermosaic.com*
CAREERPATH: *www.careerpath.com*
CAREER RESOURCE CENTER:
   http://cgi.pathfinder.com/fortune/careers/index.html
CAREER SHOP: *www.careershop.com*
CAREERSITE: *www.careersite.com*
CAREERWEB: *www.careerweb.com*
CAREER WOMEN: *www.careerwomen.com*
CAREERS.WSJ.COM: *www.careers.wsj.com*
CLASSIFIEDS2000: *www.classifieds2000.com*
CLASSIFIED WAREHOUSE: *www.adone.com*
COLLEGE GRAD JOB HUNTER: *www.collegegrad.com*
   CONTRACT EMPLOYMENT WEEKLY:
      www.ceweekly.com
      COOL WORKS: *www.coolworks.com*
      E-SPAN'S JOBOPTIONS:
         www.joboptions.com
         4WORK: *www.4work.com*
         HEADHUNTER: *www.headhunter.net*

HEART: CAREER CONNECTION: *www.career.com*
THE HELP-WANTED NETWORK:
   www.help-wanted.net
HOT JOBS: *www.hotjobs.com*
INTERNET CAREER CONNECTION: *www.iccweb.com*
THE INTERNET JOB LOCATOR: *www.joblocator.com*
THE INTERNET JOB SOURCE: *www.statejobs.com*
THE INTERNET'S EMPLOYMENT RESOURCE:
   www.tier21.com
JOBDIRECT: *www.jobdirect.com*
JOBEXCHANGE: *www.jobexchange.com*
JOBFIND: *www.jobfind.com*
JOBHUNT: *www.job-hunt.org*
JOBS.COM: *www.jobs.com*
JOB-SEARCH-ENGINE: *www.jobsearchengine.com*
JOBTRAK: *www.jobtrak.com*
JOBVERTISE: *www.jobvertise.com*
JOBWEB: *www.jobweb.com*
THE LATPRO PROFESSIONAL NETWORK:
   www.latpro.com
MBA FREEAGENTS.COM: *www.mbafreeagents.com*
MONSTER.COM: *www.monster.com*
NET-TEMPS: *www.net-temps.com*
PASSPORTACCESS: *www.passportaccess.com*
PHILLIPS CAREER CENTER:
   www.phillips.com/careercenter.htm
RECRUITING-LINKS.COM: *www.recruiting-links.com*
WESTECH VIRTUAL JOB FAIR: *www.vjf.com*

JOB OPENINGS—ASIA
ASIA NET: *www.asia-net.com*

JOB OPENINGS—AUSTRALIA
AUSTRALIAN JOB SEARCH:
   http://jobsearch.deetya.gov.au

BYRON EMPLOYMENT AUSTRALIA:
  http://employment.byron.com.au

JOB OPENINGS—CANADA
CANADIAN JOBS CATALOGUE: www.kenevacorp.mb.ca

JOB OPENINGS—EUROPE
OVERSEAS JOBS EXPRESS: www.overseasjobs.com

JOB OPENINGS—INDIA
CAREER INDIA: www.careerindia.com
JOB OPENINGS—IRELAND
THE IRISH JOBS PAGE: www.exp.ie

JOB OPENINGS—UNITED KINGDOM
JOBSITE GROUP: www.jobsite.co.uk
VACANCIES: www.vacancies.ac.uk
WORKWEB: www.workweb.co.uk

JOB OPENINGS—UNITED STATES
ALASKA JOBS CENTER:
  www.ilovealaska.com/alaskajobs
AMERICA'S TV JOB NETWORK: www.tvjobnet.com
BOSTON.COM: www.boston.com
BOSTON JOB BANK: www.bostonjobs.com
BOSTONSEARCH: www.bostonsearch.com
THE CALIFORNIA JOB SOURCE:
  www.statejobs.com/ca.html
CAREERBOARD: www.careerboard.com
CAREERGUIDE: www.careerguide.com
CAREERLINK: www.careerlink.org/index.htm
CAROLINASCAREERWEB: www.carolinascareerweb.com
CLASSIFIND NETWORK: www.classifind.com
COLORADOJOBS: www.coloradojobs.com
FLORIDA CAREER LINK: www.floridacareerlink.com
HOUSTONCHRONICLE: www.chron.com
JOBNET: www.jobnet.com
KANSAS JOB-BANK: http://entkdhr.ink.org/kjb/index.html

MINNESOTA JOBS: www.minnesotajobs.com
NEW ENGLAND OPPORTUNITY NOCS:
  www.opnocs.org
NEW JERSEY ONLINE: www.nj.com
ONLINE COLUMBIA: www.onlinecolumbia.com
ORANGE COUNTY REGISTER:
  www.ocregister.com/ads/classified/index.shtml
PHILADELPHIA ONLINE: www.phillynews.com
THE SILICON VALLEY JOB SOURCE:
  www.valleyjobs.com
680CAREERS: www.680careers.com
STL DIRECT: http://directory.st-louis.mo.us
TOWNONLINE: www.townonline.com/working
TRIANGLE JOBS: www.trianglejobs.com
VIRGINIA EMPLOYMENT COMMISSION:
  www.vec.state.va.us
WASHINGTON EMPLOYMENT WEB PAGES:
  http://members.aol.com/gwattier/washjob.htm
WISCONSIN JOBNET: www.dwd.state.wi.us/jobnet

INDUSTRY-SPECIFIC JOB OPENINGS
—ACCOUNTING/BANKING/FINANCE—
ACCOUNTING & FINANCE JOBS:
  www.accountingjobs.com
ACCOUNTING.COM: www.accounting.com
ACCOUNTING NET: www.accountingnet.com
AMERICAN BANKER ONLINE'S CAREERZONE:
  www.americanbanker.com/careerzone
BLOOMBERG: www.bloomberg.com
CFO'S FEATURED JOBS:
  www.cfonet.com/html/cfojobs.html
FINANCIAL, ACCOUNTING,
  AND INSURANCE JOBS PAGE:
  www.nationjob.com/financial
FINCAREER: www.fincareer.com
JOBS FOR BANKERS ONLINE: www.bankjobs.com
NATIONAL BANKING NETWORK:
  www.banking-financejobs.com

—ADVERTISING/MARKETING/PUBLIC RELATIONS—
ADWEEK ONLINE: www.adweek.com
DIRECT MARKETING WORLD: www.dmworld.com
MARKETING JOBS: www.marketingjobs.com

—AEROSPACE—
AVIATION AND AEROSPACE JOBS PAGE:
    www.nationjob.com/aviation
AVIATION EMPLOYMENT:
    www.aviationemployment.com
SPACE JOBS: www.spacejobs.com

—ARTS AND ENTERTAINMENT—
THE INTERNET MUSIC PAGES: www.musicpages.com
ONLINE SPORTS:
    www.onlinesports.com/pages/CareerCenter.html

—BIOTECHNOLOGY/ SCIENTIFIC—
BIO ONLINE: www.bio.com
SCIENCE PROFESSIONAL NETWORK:
    www.recruitsciencemag.org

—CHARITIES AND SOCIAL SERVICES—
THE NONPROFIT TIMES ONLINE:
    www.nptimes.com/classified.html
SOCIALSERVICE: www.socialservice.com
SOCIAL WORK AND SOCIAL SERVICES JOBS
    ONLINE: www.gwbweb.wustl.edu/jobs/index.html

—COMMUNICATIONS—
    AIRWAVES MEDIA WEB:
        www.airwaves.com/job.html

THE JOBZONE:
    www.internettelephony.com/JobZone/jobzone.asp

—COMPUTERS—
COMPUTER:
    www.computer.org/computer/career/career.htm
THE COMPUTER JOBS STORE:
    www.computerjobs.com
COMPUTERWORK: www.computerwork.com
DICE: www.dice.com
DIGITAL CAT'S HUMAN RESOURCE CENTER:
    www.jobcats.com
IDEAS JOB NETWORK: www.ideasjn.com
I-JOBS: www.1-jobs.com
JOBS FOR PROGRAMMERS: www.prgjobs.com
JOBS.INTERNET.COM: http://jobs.internet.com
JOB WAREHOUSE: www.jobwarehouse.com
MACTALENT: www.mactalent.com
SELECTJOBS: www.selectjobs.com
TECHIES: www.techies.com

—EDUCATION—
ACADEMIC EMPLOYMENT NETWORK:
    www.academploy.com
ACADEMIC POSITION NETWORK: www.apnjobs.com
AECT PLACEMENT CENTER:
    www.aect.org/employment/employment.htm
THE CHRONICLE OF HIGHER EDUCATION/
    CAREER NETWORK: http://chronicle.com/jobs
DAVE'S ESL CAFE: www.eslcafe.com
HIGHEREDJOBS ONLINE: www.higheredjobs.com
JOBS IN HIGHER EDUCATION:
    www.gslis.utexas.edu/~acadres/jobs/index.html
LIBRARY & INFORMATION SCIENCE JOBSEARCH:
    www.carousel.lis.uiuc.edu/~jobs
THE PRIVATE SCHOOL EMPLOYMENT NETWORK:
    www.privateschooljobs.com
TEACHER JOBS: www.teacherjobs.com

—ENGINEERING—
ENGINEERJOBS: *www.engineerjobs.com*

—ENVIRONMENTAL—
ECOLOGIC:
   www.rpi.edu/dept/union/pugwash/ecojobs.htm
ENVIRONMENTAL JOBS SEARCH PAGE!:
   http://ourworld.compuserve.com/homepages/
   ubikk/env4.htm
WATER ENVIRONMENT WEB: *www.wef.org*

—GOVERNMENT—
CORPORATE GRAY ONLINE: *www.greentogray.com*
FEDERAL JOBS CENTRAL: *www.fedjobs.com*
FEDERAL JOBS DIGEST: *www.jobsfed.com*
FEDWORLD FEDERAL JOB ANNOUNCEMENT
   SEARCH: *www.fedworld.gov/jobs/jobsearch.html*
THE POLICE OFFICERS INTERNET DIRECTORY:
   www.officer.com/jobs.htm

—HEALTH CARE—
HEALTH CAREER WEB: *www.healthcareerweb.com*
HEALTH CARE JOBS ONLINE: *www.hcjobsonline.com*
HEALTH CARE RECRUITMENT ONLINE:
   www.healthcarerecruitment.com
MEDHUNTERS: *www.medhunters.com*
MEDICAL-ADMART: *www.medical-admart.com*
MEDICAL DEVICE LINK: *www.devicelink.com/career*
MEDZILLA: *www.medzilla.com*
NURSING SPECTRUM CAREER FITNESS ONLINE:
   www.nursingspectrum.com
PHYSICIANS EMPLOYMENT: *www.physemp.com*
SALUDOS HISPANIS WEB CAREER CENTER:
   www.saludos.com/cguide/hcguide.html

—HOTELS AND RESTAURANTS—
ESCOFFIER ONLINE:
   www.escoffier.com/nonscape/employ.shtml

HUMAN RESOURCES/ RECRUITING
HR WORLD: *www.hrworld.com*
JOBS 4 HR: *www.jobs4hr.com*

—INSURANCE—
THE INSURANCE CAREER CENTER:
   www.connectyou.com/talent
INSURANCE NATIONAL SEARCH:
   www.insurancerecruiters.com/insjobs/jobs.htm

—LEGAL—
LAW NEWS NETWORK: *www.lawjobs.com*
THE LEGAL EMPLOYMENT SEARCH SITE:
   www.legalemploy.com
RIGHT OF WAY EMPLOYMENT JOBLINE:
   www.rightofway.com/jobline.html

—MINING/GAS/PETROLEUM—
OIL-LINK: *www.oillink.com*

—PRINTING AND PUBLISHING—
JOBLINK FOR JOURNALISTS:
   http://ajr.newslink.org/newjoblink.html
JOBS IN JOURNALISM:
   http://eb.journ.latech.edu/jobs.html

—TRANSPORTATION—
INTERNATIONAL SEAFRERS EXCHANGE:
   www.jobxchange.com/xisetoc.com
1-800-DRIVERS:
   http://204.32.45.41/final/seek.htm

—RETAIL—
RETAIL JOBNET: *www.retailjobnet.com*

—UTILITIES—
POWER: *www.powermag.com*

Meta-List

This is a "list of lists" found on the Web, with links to sites and other Internet resources on a particular subject, like job hunting. These lists are good time-savers—they generally include a short description or review of the site or service, so you won't waste time visiting irrelevant or low-quality sites. To access a particular site, you need only click on the site name.

Meta-Lists

Also, check out some job-related meta-lists, which contain links to other on-line career resources. The Career Resource Center *www.careers.org* contains thousands of links, broken down into categories like financial services or computers and engineering. Other meta-lists to consult include Stanford University's JobHunt *www.job-hunt.org* and Purdue University's Center for Career Opportunities Sites for Job Seekers and Employers *www.purdue.edu/student/jobsites.htm.* The Riley Guide *www.dbm.com/jobguide* is another superb source of job-related resources on the Web.

Keyword Search

Another way to find job listings on the Web is to perform a keyword search in a search engine like Yahoo! or Lycos. Try using keywords like "employment opportunities," "job listings," or "positions available." Finally, a company's Web page is often an excellent source for job listings.

Commercial On-line Services

These services, which charge users to access their resources, are more recognizable by their brand names: America Online, CompuServe, Microsoft Network, and Prodigy. All these services provide users with full access to the Internet and the vast employment resources available there. America Online (AOL) and CompuServe are the two largest services and, not surprisingly, have the most resources to offer job seekers.

America Online is considered by many to have the strongest and largest collection of job listings available through a commercial on-line service. CompuServe has dozens of high-quality professional discussion groups that are ideal for networking, as well as a number of searchable business databases that offer in-depth information on tens of thousands of companies. Microsoft has worked to get into the game through acquisitions and partnerships with various Internet software companies, and Prodigy also has several quality resources worth checking out. The smaller services—like Delphi and

Genie—lack the quantity of resources presently found on AOL or CompuServe.

The following overview indicates the strengths and weaknesses of each service. To find out how to sign up with a service, visit the Web address listed.

America Online *www.aol.com* is the largest commercial on-line service, with more than 17 million households. America Online is well known for its wide range of home and leisure activities for the entire family. Since the creation of the on-line Career Center in 1989, AOL has been the leader among commercial on-line services in the resources it offers job seekers. AOL's employment databases contain thousands of job listings, all of which use the same fairly simple search engine. These listings can be accessed with the keyword "Career Center." For on-line newspapers, click on "Local Resources"; for federal opportunities, click on "Find a Job," then select a relevant site from the WorkPlace site.

CompuServe *www.compuserve.com* was purchased by America Online in 1998, yet it remains a separate and distinct service. A large portion of CompuServe's two and a half million subscribers are businesses, which is a good indication of the service's orientation. CompuServe has by far the best collection of business resources on-line, including dozens of business-related databases. Job listings are not the primary reason most job seekers like CompuServe. CompuServe's strengths lie in its research capabilities and professional forums—over nine hundred special groups for people of like ideas and interests to gather and exchange information.

The Microsoft Network *http://home.microsoft.com* has certainly drawn lots of new subscribers due to the popularity of Microsoft's Windows 95 and 98 operating systems. MSN Members will want to check out its Career Forum, which features a wealth of job search and career advice, tutorials, and information. Specialized forums include those devoted to nursing and theater professions.

In addition to these major services, the following two services are worth mentioning here—although keep in mind that they were once somewhat more prominent than they are today.

On-line Strategies

Know what you want to accomplish before you go on-line. Have an agenda prepared, complete with keywords to search for, or the names and addresses of sites you want to visit. This will save you time and money, because you won't be fumbling around on-line for the right keyword or address. Also, having a plan will lessen the chances that you'll get sidetracked into a discussion group.

On the Web, use search engines like Yahoo!, Excite, and Alta Vista to help you find what you need.

(continued on next page)

Delphi *www.delphi.com* allows free access to its many forums. Searching the "Business/Finance" forums will lead you to a number of career-related forums, though few have job listings. These forums are best used for networking, finding the occasional job lead, or staying up-to-date on discussions in different fields.

Prodigy *www.prodigy.com* was best known in the past as the favorite on-line service of families with young children, mainly because of its educational resources and games. Today, Prodigy's greatest asset is the easy Internet access it provides for its subscribers. Users can easily switch between Prodigy's services, the Web, Usenet newsgroups, and Gopher. Plus, Prodigy's main menu even contains some hypertext links to Prodigy-sponsored Web sites. *Note:* Prodigy offers *Prodigy Classic*, which provides a wide variety of member services, and *Prodigy Internet*, which is distinguished primarily by its faster and more complete access to the Internet, via partnership with Microsoft's Internet Explorer. Prodigy's Career Channel is a good example of the service's ability to incorporate the World Wide Web into a traditional on-line service.

Usenet Newsgroups

Usenet newsgroups are one of the oldest and most misunderstood areas of the Internet. What was once the exclusive territory of this country's brain trust—academics, scientists, and top government officials—has developed into one of the most popular means of exchanging information on the Internet. At the same time, many new users are scared off by what they perceive as an intimidating Usenet culture. But by ignoring the discussion groups on Usenet, you could miss out on hundreds of potential job opportunities.

Getting Started

Usenet newsgroups are accessible either through your Internet carrier or commercial on-line services. In America Online, try keyword: Newsgroups. If you have a regular Internet connection, you'll need the help of a newsreader, like Trumpet Newsreader, to organize the thousands of available newsgroups and allow you to read and post messages. Many Web browsers, like Netscape Navigator,

have a built-in newsreader. Netscape's newsreader is called Netscape News. If you can't find a newsreader on your system, call your Internet provider and ask where to find one.

Once you're in Usenet, read the messages in the newsgroups news.newusers.questions and news.announce.newusers. You'll find answers to the most commonly asked questions regarding Usenet, or you can post your own questions about Usenet. You can also find information like a history of the Internet, rules for posting messages, and hints about the Usenet writing style.

This Is a Test

After reviewing the basics of Usenet, post a test message to the newsgroups alt.test or misc.tests. This test allows you to check whether your newsreader is configured properly. If you can't post test messages, ask your Internet carrier or commercial service provider for assistance. If your test goes off without a hitch, you're all set.

A Few Basic Facts

Before you begin posting messages to dozens of newsgroups on the Web, you need to know a few basic facts about Usenet. Different hierarchies and newsgroups have different tones to their discussions. In general, *alt.* newsgroups are more casual, while the *comp.* and *sci.* newsgroups are more formal and factual. And *talk.* newsgroups discuss serious subjects in a serious manner. It's important to take the time—at least one week—to get a feel for a newsgroup. This can usually be done simply by reading a few days' worth of messages. Doing this should decrease your chances of posting an inappropriate message.

Bulletin Board Systems

Bulletin Board Systems are an often overlooked on-line resource for job listings. These days, it seems everyone is more interested in the Web and services like CareerMosaic. But job-related bulletin boards can contain up to 10,000 job listings, and Bulletin Board Systems are much easier to connect to than the Web is.

(continued from previous page)

Try going on-line during off-peak hours, either early morning or late night. Services experience less traffic at these times, so it can be much easier to get through. And be sure you're dialing into a local phone number, to save money on your phone bill.

Don't rely on one particular area of the on-line world for all your job information. The Web is glamorous, but don't forget those old reliables like Usenet newsgroups and Bulletin Board Systems, as well as off-line options like joblines and directories. After you spend some time exploring, you'll probably discover that certain resources work best for you. Narrow your efforts to those areas.

Tech and Fed Jobs on BBS

Job seekers interested in finding technical positions or jobs in federal, state, or local governments should take special note of the number of BBSs dedicated to those areas.

Basically, a BBS is a computer set up with special software that you access by using a telephone line and the communications software on your computer. BBSs were created as a way for people to exchange information and discuss ideas, much like a Usenet newsgroup. Usenet newsgroups, unlike BBSs, require Internet access.

The biggest problem with BBSs is the difficulty in searching for particular boards. To dial up a BBS, you need to have the phone number beforehand for the specific board you want to access. Unlike the Web, you can't connect to a general BBS and do a search for specific BBSs by name or keyword. If you have access to the Web, try a search engine like Yahoo! or a commercial on-line service like America Online to find bulletin boards in your area. Another good resource is the BBS Corner at *http://www.thedirectory.org/diamond/bbslists.htm*

After connecting to a new BBS, you'll be required to register to use the services. This helps to discourage casual users from tying up the phone lines. Since most BBSs have a limited number of phone lines (some may have only four or five), the system operators, or sysops, limit the number of minutes users can spend on the system in one day. The systems listed here allow a maximum of one hour per day.

BBSs of job listings are quickly becoming a thing of the past. The most reliable sites are maintained by the federal government and are also available on the Web.

Exec-PC (414-789-4210)—This is an enormous BBS, with thousands of files available for download, including job listings nationwide. Also contains local access numbers for users dialing long-distance.

Federal Job Opportunities Board (FJOB) (912-757-3125 or by Internet telnet: *telnet://jobentry.opm.gov*)—Sponsored by the U.S. Office of Personnel Management, this BBS contains federal job listings and other employment information.

OPM Mainstreet (202-606-4800)—Includes federal job listings from the Office of Personnel Management as well as access to other federal job BBSs and employment-related mailing lists and Usenet newsgroups.

Networking On-line

While some may think that top executives and industry insiders are the only people to benefit from networking, that is not the case. The development of specialized on-line discussion groups has made it easier for all job seekers to meet and interact with other professionals in the same field or industry.

Job seekers should look at three main areas as potential networking resources: Usenet newsgroups, mailing lists, and special interest groups on commercial on-line services. Gopher, Telnet, and the Web don't lend themselves well to networking, since they weren't designed for two-way communication. Newsgroups, mailing lists, and SIGs, on the other hand, were designed expressly for the purpose of disseminating and receiving information. The dozens of career-related discussion groups available cover fields like accounting, education, journalism, and microbiology.

Also keep an eye out for Web sites of industry organizations and associations. While they don't have the ability to accept posted messages, field-specific Web sites are still a good way to stay current with the latest developments in a field.

Don't expect to be besieged with job offers and contact names simply because you logged on to a professional discussion group and posted a message full of intelligence and insight. Networking on-line is a slow process, since in the on-line world, as in real life, relationships don't form overnight. It may be months before any job leads materialize. That's why it's advisable to maintain a continual presence in appropriate discussion groups, even when you're happily employed, since the opportunity of a lifetime may turn up when it's least expected.

Networking on Usenet Newsgroups

Newsgroups are a terrific place for networking, with discussion groups to suit almost every interest. They also tend to have the harshest rules of netiquette, in part because their participants are more technologically savvy than the on-line world as a whole. At the same time, their users are helpful to those who have taken the time to learn the rules.

The Meter Is Running

Remember that while these services are free, you'll be charged the cost of a regular long-distance call while connected to the BBS. Try calling during off hours to minimize your phone bill.

Advantages of On-line Networking

Discussion group participants often include human resources representatives and hiring managers, who lend their expertise by discussing the qualities they look for in employees. Many recruiters report visiting field-specific discussion groups to look for potential job candidates.

Participating in on-line discussion groups brings far greater exposure than, for instance, going to a meeting of a local industry group. A discussion group's audience is most often nationwide and may even include participants from around the world.

Monitoring discussion groups makes it easy to determine what skills and experiences employers are looking for. It's also a good way to find out which companies are hiring and what the hot topics are in the field.

The following are some that you should know about:

alt.journalism.moderated—Moderated discussion group for journalists

bionet.women-in-bio—Discusses issues relevant to women in the field of biology

bionet.microbiology—Discussion of issues related to microbiology

hepnet.jobs—Discussion of issues relating to high-energy nuclear physics

k12.chat.teacher—Discussion group for teachers, from kindergarten to 12th grade

misc.business.consulting—Discusses the consulting business

misc.education—General discussion of the educational system

misc.jobs.contract—Discussion of both short- and long-term contract labor

misc.jobs.misc—General issues of employment and careers

misc.legal—Discussion group for lawyers and other legal professionals

misc.writing—Discussion group for writers of all types

sci.med—Discussion group for those interested in science and medicine

sci.med.pharmacy—Discusses the pharmaceutical field

sci.research.careers—Discusses the various careers relating to scientific research

Networking with Mailing Lists

Like newsgroups, mailing lists, also known as list-serves or e-mail discussion groups, allow users to post and read messages that contain threads of discussions on various topics. What sets mailing lists apart from newsgroups is that instead of users logging in to a specific group and posting and reading messages on-line, subscribers both receive new messages and post messages to the group via e-mail. Many users like mailing lists because it's possible to monitor discussion groups simply by checking one's e-mail.

To subscribe to a mailing list, send an e-mail to the list's system administrator. The administrator makes sure all messages are sent to subscribers and moderates the content, ensuring that postings are relevant to the topic. Like other discussion groups, each

The Importance of Netiquette

"Netiquette" is a combination of the words "network" (or Internet) and "etiquette," and refers to the widely accepted do's and don'ts for on-line discussion groups. It is essential that new users, or "newbies," be familiar with the netiquette of a group before joining the discussion; otherwise, they may get "flamed" (criticized and ridiculed by established group members).

The easiest way to avoid getting flamed is to spend time observing and reading the group's posted messages before joining the discussion. Each discussion group, especially those on Usenet, have a particular tone and rules. "Lurking" (reading messages but not posting your own) will give you a good sense of the group's personality. This is also a good way to ensure that a group fits your interests.

When you're ready to join the discussion, don't simply post a general message along the lines of "Hi, I'm new here and just wanted to drop in and say hello!" Post a message asking for specific advice or introduce an original thought or comment to the discussion. A boring, generic posting with headers like "Help!" or "Hire Me!" will be ignored at best and will get you flamed at worst. If you do get flamed—something bound to happen to every new user once or twice—just ignore it. Unless you violated a sacred rule of netiquette, someone was probably just having a bad day.

Following are some other basic rules of netiquette, as well as some general guidelines for professional discussion groups:

- Write in complete sentences, and be sure spelling, punctuation, grammar, and capitalization are correct.
- Don't type messages in capital letters, because that's the on-line equivalent of SHOUTING.
- Don't use "emoticons," like :) [happy face] or : ([frown] or common abbreviations like BTW (by the way) or IMHO (in my humble opinion), which are commonly used in recreational discussion groups. These types of cutesy shorthand are out of place in a professional discussion group. For more information, visit the following sites:

www.utopiasw.demon.co.uk/emoticon.htm
www.ultranet.com/support/netiquette/
    emoticons.shtml

- Understand the appropriate times to post or e-mail a reply to a particular message. Many new and experienced users alike are often unsure of when to direct an e-mail to the message's author and when a reply should be posted to the group. In general, post a reply if your message is something the group as a whole could appreciate and learn from, but use e-mail if your comment concerns only the poster. This is important because no one wants to participate in a discussion that is little more than a dialogue between two or three people.
- Use your best manners. Respect and be tolerant of others' ideas and opinions.

mailing list has its own rules, so be sure to contact the administrator for details.

Tens of thousands of mailing lists cover subjects like arts, business, health, politics, and religion. To find the ones that match your interests, consult one of the following on-line directories. Each directory contains contact information, like the system administrator's e-mail address, for over 50,000 mailing lists.

Liszt: The Mailing List Directory *www.liszt.com* claims to be the largest directory of mailing lists, and it just may be, with 84,792 lists available for searching. The site also allows you to search by keywords.

Publicly Accessible Mailing Lists *www.neosoft.com/ internet/paml* contains hundreds of subject classifications and is searchable by name or subject. Check under "jobs" or "employment" for job-related mailing lists, but check out lists in your field as well. This list is also posted to the Usenet newsgroups news.lists and news.answers around the end of each month.

CHAPTER 7

Interviewing

At last, you've reached the long-sought goal. All your efforts spent writing the resume and cover letter, answering job listings, networking, and researching companies have paid off—you've been called for an interview! As with these previous steps, certain techniques will increase your chances of success. Follow these techniques to maximize your chances of landing the job.

Know the Company

As each interview is arranged, begin your in-depth research. You should arrive at an interview knowing the company upside down and inside out. You need to know the company's products, types of customers, subsidiaries, parent company, principal locations, rank in the industry, sales and profit trends, type of ownership, size, current plans, and much more. By this time, you've probably narrowed your job search to one industry. Even if you haven't, you should still be familiar with common industry terms, the trends in the firm's industry, the firm's principal competitors and their relative performance, and the direction in which the industry leaders are headed.

Dig into every resource you can! Surf the Internet. Read the company literature, the trade press, the business press. If possible, speak to someone at the firm before the interview, or if not, speak to someone at a competing firm. The more time you spend, the better. Even if you feel extremely pressed for time, set aside several hours for pre-interview research.

Attire

How important is proper attire for a job interview? Buying a complete wardrobe, donning new shoes, and having your hair styled every morning aren't enough to guarantee you a career position as an investment banker. On the other hand, if you can't find a clean, conservative suit or won't take the time to wash your hair, you're wasting your time by interviewing at all.

Men applying for any professional position should wear a suit, preferably in a conservative color like navy or charcoal gray. It's easy to get away with wearing the same dark suit to consecutive interviews at the same company; just wear a different shirt and tie for each interview.

Women should also wear a businesslike suit. Professionalism still dictates a suit with a skirt, rather than slacks, as proper interview garb for women. This is usually true even at companies where pants are acceptable attire for female employees.

The final selection of candidates for a job opening won't be determined by dress, but inappropriate dress can quickly eliminate a first-round candidate. So while you shouldn't spend a fortune on a new wardrobe, be sure your clothes are adequate. The key is to dress at least as formally and conservatively as the position requires, or slightly more so.

Grooming

Personal grooming is as important as finding appropriate clothes for a job interview. Careful grooming indicates both a sense of thoroughness and self-confidence. Women should not wear excessive makeup, and both men and women should refrain from wearing perfume or cologne. (It only takes a small spritz to leave an allergic interviewer with a fit of sneezing and a bad impression of your meeting.) Men should be freshly shaven, even if the interview is late in the day.

What to Bring

Everyone needs a watch, a pen, and a notepad. Finally, a briefcase or a leatherbound folder (containing extra, unfolded copies of your resume) will help complete the look of professionalism.

Sometimes the interviewer will be running behind schedule. Don't be upset—be sympathetic. Recruiters are often under pressure to interview a lot of candidates to quickly fill a demanding position. Come to your interview with good reading material to keep yourself occupied and relaxed.

The Crucial First Few Moments

The beginning of the interview is the most important, because it determines the tone. Do you smile when you meet? Do you establish enough eye contact, but not too much? Do you walk into the office with a self-assured and confident stride? Do you shake hands firmly? Do you make small talk easily, without being garrulous, or do you act formal and reserved, as though under attack? It's human nature to judge people by that first impression, so make sure it's a good one.

Do you wait for the recruiter to invite you to sit down before doing so? Alternatively, if the recruiter forgets to invite you to take a seat, do you awkwardly ask if you may be seated, as though to remind the recruiter of a lapse in etiquette? Or do you gracefully help yourself to a seat? As you can see, much of the first impression you make at an interview will be dramatically affected by how relaxed and confident you feel. This is why it's important to practice for each interview.

Avoid the Negative

Try not to be negative about anything during the interview, particularly any past employer or previous job. Even if you detest your current or former job or manager, don't make disparaging comments. The interviewer may construe this as a sign of a potential attitude problem and not consider you a strong candidate.

Take some time to really think about how you'll convey your work history. Present "bad experiences" as "learning experiences." Instead of saying "I hated my position as a salesperson because I had to bother people on the phone," say "I realized cold-calling wasn't my strong suit. Though I love working with people, I decided my talents would be best used in a more face-to-face atmosphere." Always find some sort of lesson from previous jobs, as they all have one.

Money: Don't Ask

It's usually best to avoid talking finances until you receive the offer. Otherwise you'll look like you care more about money than putting your skills to work for the company. Your goals at an interview are simple: 1) to prove to the recruiter that you're well-suited to the job

as you understand it, and 2) to make sure you feel comfortable with the prospect of actually doing the job and working in the environment the company offers. Even if you're unable to determine the salary range beforehand, don't ask about it during the first interview. You can always ask later. Above all, don't ask about fringe benefits until you've been offered a position. (Then be sure to get all the details.)

If you're pressed about salary requirements during an interview and you feel you must name a figure, give a salary range instead of your most recent salary. Naming a salary range gives you a chance to hook onto a figure that's also in the range the company has in mind. In fact, many companies base their offers on sliding salary scales. Therefore, if you name a range of, say, $25,000–30,000, it may be that the company was considering a range of $22,000–28,000. In this case, you'll be more likely to receive an offer in the mid-to-upper end of your range. Of course, your experience and qualifications also play a part here. If you're just starting out and have little experience, the recruiter may be more likely to stick to the lower end of the scale.

Handling Impossible Questions

One of the biggest fears candidates harbor about job interviews is the unknown question for which they have no answer. To make matters worse, some recruiters may ask a question knowing full well you can't answer it. They don't usually ask such questions because they enjoy seeing you squirm—they want to judge how you might respond to pressure or tension on the job. If you're asked a tough question you can't answer, think about it for a few seconds. Then, with a confident smile and without apology, simply say "I don't know" or "I can't answer that question."

You'll find some of the toughest of these questions later in the chapter, under "Zingers."

After the Interview

You've made it through the toughest part—but now what? First, breathe a sigh of relief! Then record the name and title of the person you interviewed with, as well as the names and titles of anyone else you may have met. Ideally, you'll have collected their business cards. Don't forget to write down what the next agreed-upon step will be. Will the recruiter contact you? How soon?

Don't Forget to Write

Write a follow-up letter immediately afterward, while the interview is still fresh in the interviewer's mind. Not only is this a thank-you, it also gives you the chance to provide the interviewer with any details you may have forgotten (as long as they can be added tactfully). If you lost any points during the interview, this letter can help you regain your footing. Be polite and make sure to stress your continued interest and competence to fill the position. Just don't forget to proofread it thoroughly. If you're unsure of the spelling of the interviewer's name, call the receptionist and ask.

Handling Rejection

Rejection is inevitable, and it's bound to happen to you, just as it happens to all other job seekers. The key is to be prepared for it and not take it personally.

One way you can turn rejection around is by contacting each person who sends you a rejection letter. Thank your contact for considering you for the position and request that he or she keep you in mind for future openings. If you feel comfortable about it, you may want to ask the person for suggestions to help you improve your chances of getting a job in that industry or for the names of people who might be looking for someone with your skills—something like "Do you have any suggestions about whom else I might contact?"

Two cautions are in order: First, don't ask employers to tell you why they didn't hire you. Not only will this place a recruiter in an awkward position, you'll probably get a negative reaction. Second, keep in mind that if you contact employers solely for impartial feedback, not everyone will be willing to talk to you.

Zingers!

Following are some of the most challenging questions you'll ever face. If you're able to answer these questions, you'll be prepared to handle just about anything the recruiter comes up with.

Tell me about yourself.

I'm a production assistant with a B.A. in communications and three years of solid broadcasting and public-relations experience. I have extensive experience developing and researching topics, preinterviewing guests, and producing on-location videotapings. I have a tremendous amount of energy and love to be challenged. I'm constantly trying to take on additional responsibilities and learn new things. I've been watching your station for some time now, and I've been impressed with your innovative approach and your fast growth. I'd like to be a part of that winning team.

This is a perfect opportunity to "sell" your qualifications to the interviewer. Develop the sales messages that you want to convey, and condense them into a summary you can use in situations like this. Briefly describe your experience, skills, accomplishments, goals, and personal qualities. Explain your interest in the company and how you plan on making a contribution. If you're a recent college graduate, be sure to discuss your educational qualifications as well, emphasizing the classes you took that are relevant to the position.

What is your biggest weakness?

I admit to being a bit of a perfectionist. I take a great deal of pride in my work and am committed to producing the highest-quality work I can. Sometimes if I'm not careful, though, I can go a bit overboard. I've learned that it's not always possible or even practical to try to perfect your work—sometimes you have to decide what's important and ignore the rest to be productive. It's a question of trade-offs. I also pay a lot of attention to pacing my work, so I don't get too caught up in perfecting every detail.

If Your Skills Aren't Appropriate . . .

If it looks as though your skills and background don't match the position the interviewer was hoping to fill, ask him or her if another division or subsidiary could perhaps profit from your talents.

This is a great example of what's known as a negative question. Negative questions are a favorite among interviewers, because they're effective at uncovering problems or weaknesses. The key to answering negative questions is to give them a positive spin. For this particular question, your best bet is to admit to a weakness that isn't catastrophic, inconsistent, or currently disruptive to your chosen professional field, and emphasize how you've overcome or minimized it. Whatever you do, don't answer this question with a cop-out like "I can't think of any" or, even worse, "I don't really have any major weaknesses." This kind of response is likely to eliminate you from contention.

Tell me about a project in which you were disappointed with your personal performance.

In my last job for a manufacturing company, I had to analyze all the supplier bids and present recommendations to the vice president of logistics. Because the supplier bids weren't in a uniform format, my analysis often consisted of comparing dissimilar items. This caused some confusion in my final report, and by the time I'd reworked it and presented it to the vice president, we'd lost the critical time we needed to improve our approval process for these bids. In hindsight, I should have taken a simpler approach to the problem and not tried to make it so complex or all-inclusive. Ever since, I've paid more attention to making recommendations in a timely manner.

Describe roadblocks and what you've done to try to get around them. How have your skills come into play? In hindsight, what could you have done differently? What lessons have you learned?

What aspects of your work are most often criticized?

I remember in my first job as marketing assistant, I spent endless hours analyzing a particular problem. I came up with a revised marketing plan that was extremely well received. Unfortunately, when it came time to present the plan to top management, I hadn't prepared the fine points of the presentation— overheads and slides—and the proposal was turned down. I'd failed to make clear the savings that would result from the plan. I spent the next two weeks working on my presentation. On my second try management approved it, and my recommendations were carried out to everyone's satisfaction.

This question is similar to the question on weaknesses. Try to give an example from a job early on in your career. Discuss what you did to overcome the situation and to improve your work. You could also discuss how the failure has inspired you to pay more careful attention to detail in all your work.

Why did you stay in your last job so long?

I was in my last job over seven years. During that time, I completed an advanced technical degree at an evening university and also had two six-month assignments in which I was loaned out to different departments. As a result, I acquired some additional skills that normally aren't associated with that job. Therefore, I think I've made good progress and am ready to accept the next challenge.

The interviewer may be curious about your interest in personal improvement, tackling new assignments, and so on. He or she may also be concerned about whether you have a tendency to get too comfortable with the status quo. Demonstrate how you've developed job responsibilities in meaningful new ways.

Would you be willing to relocate to another city?

I'd prefer to be based here, but it's certainly a possibility I'd be willing to consider.

You may, even in some first interviews, be asked questions that seem to elicit a tremendous commitment on your behalf, like this one. Although such questions may be unfair during an initial job interview, you may well conclude that you have nothing to gain and everything to lose with a negative response. If you're asked such a question unexpectedly during an initial job interview, simply say something like

Skirt versus Pants for Women

For those women who are still convinced that pants are acceptable interview attire, listen to the words of one career counselor from a prestigious New England college: "I had a student who told me that since she knew women in her industry often wore pants to work, she was going to wear pants to her interviews. Almost every recruiter commented that her pants were 'too casual' and even referred to her as 'the one with the pants.' The funny thing was that one of the recruiters who commented on her pants had been wearing jeans!"

"That's certainly a possibility" or "I'm willing to consider that." Later, if you receive an offer, you can find out the specific conditions and then decide if you wish to accept the position. Remember, at the job-offer stage you have the most negotiating power, and the employer may be willing to accommodate your needs. If that isn't the case, you might wish to explain that upon reflection, you've decided you can't (for instance) relocate, but you'd like to be considered for other positions that might open up in the future.

Why should I hire you?

I offer over five years of expertise in management, including electronic assembly for a major computer manufacturer and injection-molding operations for a prominent plastics company. Because I have the ability to adjust and learn new skills quickly, I've often been called upon to start new operations. I'm confident, on the basis of my skills and experience, that I can help improve production by leading a team effort directed at achieving your company's goals.

You'll usually encounter this question toward the end of a job interview; how you answer it can make or break your candidacy. Instead of reiterating your resume, emphasize only a few of your strongest qualifications and relate them to the position in question.

What would you do if I told you I thought you were giving a very poor interview today?

Well, the first thing I'd do is ask you if there was any part of the interview you thought I mishandled. After that, I'd think back and try to remember if there had been any faulty communication on my part. Then I'd try to review possible problems I had understanding your questions, and I'd ask for clarification if I needed it. Finally, if we had time, I'd try to respond more fully and appropriately to the problem areas you identified for me.

Interviewers like to ask stress questions like these to see how well you hold up under pressure. Your best bet is to stay calm, relaxed, and don't allow your confidence to be shaken.

Sometimes recruiters ask seemingly impossible questions just to see how you'll respond. No matter how you may feel at the time, being subjected to a ridiculous question like this one is probably a good sign. If you're asked a tough question that you can't answer, think about it for a few seconds. Then, with a confident smile, simply say something like "I don't know, but if you hire me, I'll sure find out for you."

Illegal Questions

Illegal interview questions probe into your private life or personal background. Federal law forbids employers from discriminating against any person on the basis of sex, age, race, national origin, or religion. For instance, an interviewer may not ask you about your age or your date of birth. However, she or he may ask you if you're over eighteen years of age. If you're asked an illegal question at a job interview, keep in mind that many employers simply don't know what's legal and illegal.

One strategy in such cases is to try to discover the concerns behind the question and then address them. For instance, an employer who asks about your plans to have children may be concerned that you won't be able to fulfill the travel requirements of the position. Try to get to the heart of the issue by saying something like "I'm not quite sure I understand." If you can determine the interviewer's concerns, you can allay them with a reply like "I'm very interested in developing my career. Travel is definitely not a problem for me—in fact, I enjoy it tremendously."

Alternatively, you may choose to answer the question or to gracefully point out that the question is illegal and decline to respond. Avoid reacting in a hostile fashion—remember that you can always decide later to decline a job offer.

Any of the following responses is an acceptable way to handle these situations. Choose the response that's most comfortable for you, keeping in mind that adhering to your principles may cost you the job.

Bring a Good Book

The Corporate Controller at one large company makes everyone wait for at least one hour before he will interview them. He feels his time is more valuable than anyone else's. This is where you have to ask yourself: "How much do I really want this job—especially if I have to report to this person?"

What religion do you practice?

Answer 1: I make it a point not to mix my personal beliefs with my work, if that's what you mean. I assure you that I value my career too much for that.

Answer 2: I'm not quite sure I understand what you're getting at. Would you please explain to me how this issue is relevant to the position?

Answer 3: That question makes me uncomfortable. I'd really rather not answer it.

How old are you?

Answer 1: I'm in my fifties and have over thirty years of experience in this industry. My area of expertise is in . . .

Answer 2: I'm not quite sure I understand what you're getting at. Would you please explain to me how this issue is relevant to the position?

Answer 3: That question makes me uncomfortable. I'd really rather not answer it.

Are you married?

Answer 1: No.

Answer 2: Yes, I am. But I keep my family life separate from my work life so that I can put all my effort into my job. I'm flexible when it comes to travel and late hours, as my references can confirm.

Answer 3: I'm not quite sure I understand what you're getting at. Would you please explain to me how this issue is relevant to the position?

Answer 4: That question makes me uncomfortable. I'd really rather not answer it.

Do you have children?

Answer 1: No.

Answer 2: Yes, I do. But I keep my family life separate from my work life so that I can put all my effort into my job. I'm flexible when it comes to travel and late hours, as my references can confirm.

Answer 3: I'm not quite sure I understand what you're getting at. Would you please explain to me how this issue is relevant to the position?

Answer 4: That question makes me uncomfortable. I'd really rather not answer it.

Do you plan to have children?

Answer 1: No.

Answer 2: It's certainly a consideration, but if I do, it won't be for some time. I want to do the best job I can for this company and have no plans to leave just as I begin to make meaningful contributions.

Answer 3: I can't answer that right now. But if I ever do decide to have children, I wouldn't let it detract from my work. Becoming a parent is important, but my career is certainly important to me, too. I plan on putting all of my efforts into this job and this company.

Answer 4: I'm not quite sure I understand what you're getting at. Would you please explain to me how this issue is relevant to the position?

Answer 5: That question makes me uncomfortable. I'd really rather not answer it.

For Students and Recent Graduates

Being So Positive That It Hurts

Many inexperienced job candidates kill their chances for a job by making negative comments during an interview. A college student or recent grad should never make a negative statement about a former boss or teacher—even if it's completely true and fully justified. If the recruiter asks why you had an unsatisfactory grade in a particular course, don't say "The professor graded me unfairly" or "I didn't get along with the professor."

A recruiter would rather hire someone who gets and deserves an unsatisfactory grade in a course than someone who either doesn't get along with people or shifts blame to others. On the other hand, you can greatly increase your chances of getting any job by projecting a positive, upbeat attitude. This is one of the best ways to stand out from the competition. You can project this image by smiling from time to time during the interview; by responding to interview questions with enthusiasm; by demonstrating excitement about your past accomplishments; and by showing optimism about the prospect of starting your career.

Commonly Asked Questions

Whether you're graduating from high school or college, those of you with little or no work history face the same dilemma: it's tough to get a job without experience, and it seems impossible to gain experience without getting hired. But, as you'll see, there are ways to get around this problem—by emphasizing your strengths and educational achievements.

The following responses to interview questions are listed as examples to show you how questions should be handled. They should not be used as the basis of "canned" or scripted answers. Adapt these responses for your own circumstances, but remember that, especially for college students or recent grads, how an answer is given can be more important than what's said. Be positive, project confidence, smile and make eye contact with the interviewer, listen carefully, and go with the flow!

About School Grades

It's likely that if you've made it to the interview stage, you fulfill the basic criteria for the position, including the education requirements. The recruiter is probably trying to judge here how well the candidate handles adversity. It's important not to get defensive or to place blame. Instead, try to put a positive spin on the question—for example, by concentrating on what you learned and the extra effort you put in rather than on the grades you received.

Why are your grades so erratic?

I never hesitated to sign up for a course just because it had a reputation for being difficult. In fact, my American History professor, whose course I enjoyed tremendously, is notorious for giving out only one "A" for each class. You may have noticed that while my major is English, I did take four courses in physics, because I thought they were important to round out my education, and I enjoyed the challenge they presented. Almost everyone else in these courses was a physics major.

About Academics

What course did you find most challenging?

Initially, I was completely overwhelmed by the introductory chemistry course I took last year. No matter how hard I studied, I seemed to be getting nowhere. I failed the first three quizzes. So I tried a new approach. Instead of just studying by myself, I had a friend—a chemistry major—help me with my studies. I also began to get help after class from the professor from time to time. And I found that more time spent in the lab was critical. I ended up with a B+ in the course, and I felt I achieved a solid understanding of the material. More than that, I learned that tackling a new field of study sometimes requires a new approach, not just hard work, and that the help of others can be crucial!

The interviewer will want to see how well you respond to difficult situations. Demonstrate that you won't fold in the face of difficulty and that you're willing to put in the extra effort to meet a challenge.

Why did you decide to major in history?

It was a difficult choice, because I was also attracted to government, international relations, and economics. But the study of history allowed me to combine all three, especially since I focused on economic history. I also found several of the professors in the department exceptionally knowledgeable and stimulating.

Show that you have solid, logical reasons for choosing your major. If you can't defend your choice of major, the interviewer will wonder how much thought you've put into choosing a career. You should also be sure that your reasons for choosing your major are compatible with your career choice. For instance, if you're applying for a position as a banker, don't say you were an English major because you love literature and writing.

About Extracurricular Activities

You seem to have participated a little bit in a lot of different extracurricular activities. Didn't any of them really hold your interest?

I've always felt it was important to have a well-rounded education, and I looked at extracurricular activities as an important part of that education. That's why I participated in many different activities—to broaden my experience and meet new people. I did particularly enjoy the drama club and the cycling team, but I made a conscious effort not to spend too much time on them and to try new and different activities.

About Lack of Work Experience

I see that while you returned to your hometown each summer, you worked at different companies. Why didn't you work the same job two summers in a row?

My career goal is to get a job in business after graduation. Because I attend a liberal arts college, I can't take any courses in business. So even though I was invited back to each summer job I held, I thought I could develop more experience by working in different positions. Although I didn't list high school jobs on my resume, I did work for almost three years at the same grocery store chain.

PART TWO

COVER LETTER SAMPLES

CHAPTER 8

Special Situations

178 Green Street
Fort Worth, TX 76111
(817) 555-5555

April 11, 2001

Pat Cummings
Vice President
Any Corporation
1140 Main Street
Fort Worth, TX 76101

Dear Mr. Cummings:

Is your corporation in need of a motivated professional with comprehensive product management experience? If so, I would like to present my qualifications for your consideration.

My experience has provided me with insight into all aspects of product/protocol development and management to obtain FDA product approval. As you will note from my resume, my responsibilities as Product Manager for Estrade, Inc., involved coordinating all product development for a large medical supply corporation. My product designs and management and marketing techniques have been recognized as consistently innovative. Much of my work has involved collaboration with systems consultants on designing and implementing data management systems, including remote access.

I appreciate your consideration and look forward to speaking with you if my capabilities can be of use at Any Corporation.

Sincerely,

Chris Smith

Chris Smith

178 Green Street
Daytona Beach, FL 32115
(904) 555-5555

August 18, 2001

Pat Cummings
Vice-President, Fiscal Affairs
Any Hospital
1140 Main Street
Orlando, FL 32816

Dear Mr. Cummings:

I am in search of an opportunity in materials management within the health-care field and would like to inquire about the possibility of joining your management team.

During the past eighteen years, I have progressed rapidly in positions of responsibility from supervisor of patient transportation to manager of warehousing/distribution to my current position as senior buyer and manager of inventory control.

In the latter position, I have been able to reduce the expenditures of all in-house medical and nonmedical supplies substantially each year through cost-effective negotiations, purchasing, and control. I also played a key role in automating inventories and providing a functional layout for warehouse locations that reduced the selection and distribution process for warehoused materials. This also enabled me to provide more stringent controls, reducing shrinkage, damage, and obsolescence—common problems in the health-care field.

I look forward to hearing from you if my skills can be applied at Any Corporation.

Sincerely,

Chris Smith

Chris Smith

APPLICATION FOR IN-HOUSE POSITION
District Supervisor

178 Green Street
Big Stone Gap, VA 24219
(703) 555-5555

September 17, 2001

Pat Cummings
Personnel Director
Any Gas Company
1140 Main Street
Norfolk, VA 23510

Re: Management Job Posting
District Supervisor (Grade 25)

Dear Ms. Cummings:

In accordance with the management job posting for the above position, I enclose my resume summarizing my experience with Any Gas Company and other employers in the gas distribution industry.

All these positions required the ability to provide technical support, retain personnel, supervise outside contractors, and work with developers and public officials during the joint work programs and projects. I have the technical capability to work with and direct company and contractor personnel on all phases of gas distribution systems, from new construction to replacement and operation.

My previous accomplishments with Any Gas indicate my strong communication skills and my ability to work with people at all levels of responsibility. I feel well prepared to handle the challenges of the district supervisor position.

I look forward to meeting with you to discuss my candidacy. Thank you for your consideration.

Sincerely,

Chris Smith

Chris Smith

178 Green Street
Lexington, MA 02854
(617) 555-5555
csmith@netmail.com

July 23, 2001

Pat Cummings
Director
Any Advertising Agency
1140 Main Street
Sausalito, CA 94966

Dear Mr. Cummings:

I am seeking a freelance or part-time position in graphic design or advertising production. In addition to a Bachelor of Arts degree and current enrollment in Massachusetts College of Art's Graphic Design Certificate Program, I offer more than seven years' experience in production and traffic areas of print and graphic design and in related fields, including fundraising and direct and mass mailings.

As you can see from my resume, I left the field three years ago with excellent references to raise a family and manage a household. Now, with a family well established, I am highly motivated to return to the workforce and contribute the experience gained before and during my hiatus.

I look forward to hearing from you if my skills can be of use at Any Agency.

Sincerely,

Chris Smith

Chris Smith

178 Green Street
Daytona Beach, FL 32115
(904) 555-5555

August 18, 2001

Pat Cummings
Hiring Manager
Any Advertising Agency
1140 Main Street
Orlando, FL 32816

Dear Mr. Cummings:

I would like to inquire about the possibility of a position at your agency. I have over eight years' experience in promotion, communications, and administration.

As owner of a housecleaning service for four years, I designed and wrote all promotional materials, including direct-mail coupons. Immediately after my first promotional campaign, the volume of business tripled, resulting in my hiring six people. In addition to supervising the employees, I managed the office, which entailed handling calls, scheduling, billing, record keeping, ordering supplies, and customer relations. I found that what I enjoyed most was promotion, so I have just sold the business and am seeking a position in advertising.

In addition to my business experience, I have strong communication skills from prior employment as a teacher, which enables me to explain ideas clearly. These skills also enabled me to procure donations of computers and software from a local business and to promote school fundraising events.

I hope to hear from you if you have an opening for someone with my qualifications.

Thank you for your consideration.

Sincerely,

Chris Smith

Chris Smith

178 Green Street
Arkadelphia, AR 71999
(501) 555-5555
csmith@netmail.com

March 12, 2001

Pat Cummings
Human Resources Director
Any Corporation
1140 Main Street
Pine Bluff, AR 71601

Dear Ms. Cummings:

I am responding to your recent request in the Arkansas *Democratic-Gazette* for a business consultant.

Currently, I am a faculty member in the Department of Management and Aviation Science at Henderson State University. I am also engaged in several consulting assignments involving installation, conversion, and maintenance of automated accounting systems, troubleshooting, and training. I have taught several applications and operating systems, including spreadsheets, word processing, and accounting, in Windows, Mac, and traditional DOS environments.

In strategic market development, the ability to assess customer needs relative to overall market conditions and to respond to them rapidly is critical for successful business development. I can provide you with innovative approaches to getting the job done.

I look forward to hearing from you if I can help you increase your value-added services and profitability.

Sincerely,

Chris Smith

Chris Smith

178 Green Street
Boise, ID 83725
(208) 555-5555

August 5, 2001

Pat Cummings
Vice-President
Any Corporation
1140 Main Street
Chicago, IL 60605

Dear Ms. Cummings:

I am forwarding my resume with regard to the opening in your marketing department, as advertised in the August 4 edition of the *Chicago Tribune*.

Although I am now employed in a management position, I am interested in a career change, especially one where I can combine my thorough knowledge of boating with my sales, marketing, and communication skills. As a semiprofessional sailboat racer, I twice won national honors and participated in the races at Cape Cod. In addition, I have made lasting contacts with owners and officials.

I am confident that my business background and knowledge of boats would enable me to have a favorable impact on both your sales and image.

Thank you for your attention.

Sincerely,

Chris Smith

Chris Smith

178 Green Street
Wichita, KS 67202
(316) 555-5555

February 4, 2001

Pat Cummings
Vice-President
Any Bank
1140 Main Street
Topeka, KS 66607

Dear Ms. Cummings:

During the past eight years, I have been actively involved as vice president and director of operations of an established, quality, $1.4 million function and recreation complex, with total responsibility for creating effective sales programs and assuring the quality of services provided.

Currently, I am seeking a career change and opportunity to associate with a progressive bank, where I can effectively apply my creative and innovative talents and capability for developing or increasing new service products.

I am adept at initiating promotional advertising and marketing programs that stimulate growth and profits.

If you are in need of someone with these capabilities, I hope you will give me the opportunity to speak to you.

I appreciate your consideration.

Yours sincerely,

Chris Smith

Chris Smith

DISPLACED HOMEMAKER
Administrator

178 Green Street
Solon, OH 44139
(216) 555-5555

February 25, 2001

Pat Cummings
Human Resources Director
Any Corporation
1140 Main Street
Cleveland, OH 44111

Dear Mr. Cummings:

I would like to offer my skills and experience for your consideration regarding an administrative position at Any Corporation.

I offer extensive, varied experience in administration, including staff supervision, meeting planning and direction, and activities scheduling. I have the ability to speak effectively before groups, and I communicate well through phone contact or the written word. My skills also include fundraising, promotion, and bookkeeping.

If you are looking for someone with these skills, I hope you will give me the opportunity to speak to you.

Thank you for your time.

Sincerely,

Chris Smith

Chris Smith

178 Green Street
Pennesauken, NJ 08110
(609) 555-5555

July 23, 2001

Pat Cummings
President
Any Executive Search Firm
1140 Main Street
Pleasantville, NJ 08232

Dear Ms. Cummings:

My interest in applying for a position as a recruiter at your firm has prompted me to forward the attached professional profile for your consideration.

My expertise was gained over seven years while recruiting high technology, support staff, and marketing personnel. Much of this experience involved extensive travel, training program development, and networking prospective clients. I possess valuable contacts within the management information systems, software development, and engineering industries that would prove valuable to your client base.

I would like to apply my skills and knowledge as a member of your recruiting staff. I believe I could significantly contribute to your firm's success.

Thank you for your time.

Sincerely,

Chris Smith

Chris Smith

178 Green Street
Cambridge, MA 02142
(617) 555-5555

May 18, 2001

Pat Cummings
Director
Any Agency
1140 Main Street
Boston, MA 02118

Dear Ms. Cummings:

I read about your agency in the May edition of *Save Our Earth* and was impressed by your Stop and Think! campaign to educate Boston in choosing environmentally safe alternatives for everyday living. I wonder if you might have an opening for an environmental advocate?

I have both a passion for environmental concerns and practical experience. For the past four years, I have been operating my own business, Recycling Renegades, in Cambridge. I successfully acquired the first recycling permit in Cambridge for ferrous and nonferrous metal, aluminum, high-grade paper, and plastic. As owner and manager, I conducted research, developed pilot programs, formulated networks for voluntary recycling, picked up and processed materials, and distributed proceeds to community associations.

I now feel it is time to shift to a wider focus. I would like to apply my skills to developing innovative programs to promote all environmental concerns. Would it be possible to meet for an interview? I have several ideas I'd like to share with you.

Sincerely,

Chris Smith

Chris Smith

178 Green Street
Miami, FL 33132
(305) 555-5555

September 21, 2001

Pat Cummings
Executive Producer
Any Production Company
1140 Main Street
Hialeah, FL 33012

Dear Mr. Cummings:

I would like to apply for the production assistant position advertised in the *Miami Herald*.

I have extensive experience in all aspects of video production, including positions as writer, researcher, director, and editor. For the past three years I have been a freelance production assistant working on several commercial and documentary pieces. As chief assistant on *Milk Carton Kids: An American Crisis,* I assisted in preliminary research and writing, scheduling location shooting, and screening potential interview candidates. I also helped complete two public-service announcements for Miami Child Services, where my duties included camera operation and heavy editing.

I've admired Any Production Company's work for some time and attended your screening of *Silent Victims* at the Miami Crime Awareness Convention last month.

I look forward to hearing from you.

Sincerely,

Chris Smith

Chris Smith

FREELANCER
Writer

178 Green Street
Oklahoma City, OK 73125
(918) 555-5555
csmith@netmail.com

January 6, 2001

Pat Cummings
Publisher
Any Publishing Company
1140 Main Street
Toledo, OH 43660

Dear Ms. Cummings:

I am a freelance writer of educational and reference materials for college students and adults. My experience is primarily in the areas of careers, self-help, and parenting. Having frequently noticed such books by Any Publishing Company on the bestseller lists, I would like to learn more about your freelance needs.

My clients tell me I have a facility for synthesizing information and conveying it in a creative and well-organized way. Whether writing textbook materials, teacher apparatus, or ancillary activities and worksheets, I can tailor the tone and approach to a variety of purposes and audiences.

I wonder if I could speak to you about undertaking some of your projects? I can provide a variety of writing samples and references.

Thank you for your consideration.

Sincerely,

Chris Smith

Chris Smith

178 Green Street
Tallassee, AL 36078
(205) 555-5555

June 3, 2001

Pat Cummings
Curator
Any Museum
1140 Main Street
Mobile, AL 36633

Dear Ms. Cummings:

   I am seeking a full-time position in which I can apply both museum and gallery experience and a keen interest in fine art.

   As you will note from my resume, I have completed two extensive internships for successful art galleries in Alabama. In each position, I was exposed to all aspects of operations, from sales to clerical duties. My responsibilities included assisting customers, setting up displays, and completing mailings for exhibitions. I have a Bachelor of Arts degree in Art History, have participated in several related seminars, and have had occasion to visit many of the world's great museums.

   I hope you will give me the opportunity to discuss my qualifications further.

Sincerely,

Chris Smith

Chris Smith

178 Green Street
Provo, UT 84602
(801) 555-5555

January 10, 2001

Pat Cummings
Controller
Any Corporation
1140 Main Street
Provo, UT 84602

Dear Ms. Cummings:

During the past twelve years, my experience has been focused in transportation and sales. Seven of these years were spent with the United States Army. Although my recent experience has been in the sale of intangibles, I am interested in resuming a civilian career in transportation operations or in the sale of products or equipment allied to the transportation field.

I have a Bachelor of Science degree and am a graduate officer of the U.S. Army Transportation School—the equivalent of a graduate school. In addition to managing all phases of complete civilian and tactical transportation operations (vehicles from two-and-one-half-ton cargo trucks to ten-ton tractor trailers and petroleum tankers), I have taught courses and have trained troops in the total transportation cycle in the United States and abroad.

With my qualifications in the transportation field, I can contribute substantially toward the efficient operation of an in-house traffic, transportation, and distribution function and/or commercial transportation depot.

I would appreciate the opportunity to further discuss my qualifications in the transportation field and the immediate and long-term contribution I could make to Any Corporation.

Sincerely,

Chris Smith

Chris Smith

178 Green Street
Gallup, NM 87301
(505) 555-5555

July 21, 2001

Pat Cummings
Hiring Manager
Any Accounting Firm
1140 Main Street
Albuquerque, NM 87103

Dear Mr. Cummings:

I am seeking an entry-level position in accounting in which I can apply my expertise in both financial management and customer service. While researching area firms, I learned of Any Accounting Firm's esteemed training and development program. To such a program, I would bring the following:

- a Bachelor of Science degree, cum laude, in Finance
- four years of collections experience
- successful collection of 90 percent of the company's overdue accounts
- experience in accounts payable and accounts receivable
- knowledge of Lotus 1-2-3, Word, and accounting software

I hope you will give me the opportunity to speak to you about a position at Any Accounting Firm. Thank you for your consideration.

Sincerely,

Chris Smith

Chris Smith

178 rue Vert
Paris, France
011-331-45-55-55

January 7, 2001

Pat Cummings
Director of Human Resources
Any Corporation
1140 Main Street
New York, NY 10028

Dear Ms. Cummings:

I am looking for a new position with an international service-oriented organization that can benefit from my multilingual and organizational skills in a marketing position.

I have a Bachelor of Arts degree in French (*summa cum laude*), am fluent in French and Italian, and have strong proficiency in Spanish. I also have experience as an interpreter and translator working on international market research with the International Marketing Department at the University of Paris, Sorbonne. I concurrently worked as an administrative assistant to professors and business executives.

Since 1998, I have tutored individuals in foreign languages and English as a Second Language. I am familiar with various cultures and work well with multilingual, multicultural individuals and groups.

I will be in New York from February 14 through February 28 and wonder if it would be possible to schedule an interview for that time? I will call the week of February 5 to confirm receipt of my application.

Thank you.

Sincerely,

Chris Smith

Chris Smith

PART-TIME EMPLOYMENT HISTORY
Store Manager

178 Green Street
Brooklyn, NY 11735
(516) 555-5555

April 30, 2001

Pat Cummings
District Manager
Any Retail Chain
1140 Main Street
New York, NY 10016

Dear Ms. Cummings:

My interest in joining your staff in a full-time management position has prompted me to forward the enclosed resume.

During the past seven years, I have held progressively responsible positions in retail sales, from salesperson to manager. In my most recent position as store manager for Raintree Designs, I was responsible for an increase in branch sales from $.5 to $1.2 million in one year. I have hands-on experience in sales, inventory control, and product promotion. As assistant manager for Rips, Inc., in Brooklyn, I supervised a staff of twelve, oversaw the production of a promotional video, and assisted in selecting chain-wide promotion techniques.

As my resume indicates, the majority of my retail management experience has been part-time. I am now seeking a permanent position. I wonder if you might have need for my services at Any Retail Chain?

Thank you for your time.

Sincerely,

Chris Smith

Chris Smith

RECENT GRADUATE
Assisant Museum Director

178 Green Street
Vermillion, SD 57069
(605) 555-5555

June 26, 2001

Pat Cummings
Museum Director
Any Museum
1140 Main Street
Rapid City, SD 57701

Dear Ms. Cummings:

I am a recent graduate of the University of South Dakota with a well-rounded art history background. I would like to put my skills and knowledge to use in an entry-level position at your museum, perhaps as an assistant to the curator.

As my resume indicates, I participated in a summer program for art history majors at the Louvre. This involved studying some of the most significant works in European art and attending a seminar on the operation of the Louvre itself. I also worked for two summers at the Metropolitan Museum of Art, where I served as a museum assistant at the information booth. My coursework in African-American art, modern art, and museum science has also prepared me for a position in a fine arts museum.

I have been visiting your museum ever since I was a child and would very much like the opportunity to become part of your staff. I hope to hear from you soon.

Sincerely,

Chris Smith

Chris Smith

RECENT GRADUATE
English Teacher

178 Green Street
Plymouth, MA 02360
(508) 555-5555

April 8, 2001

Pat Cummings
Human Resources Manager
Any School District
1140 Main Street
Newton, MA 02164

Dear Mr. Cummings:

In response to last week's advertisement in the *New England Journal of Higher Education* for an English teacher, I enclose my resume for your consideration.

I have recently graduated from Boston College with a bachelor's degree in Secondary Education. I am certified to teach both English and Special Education. In addition to fulfilling my practice teaching requirement in your district, I participated in a volunteer literacy program to tutor both youth and adults struggling with reading difficulties. I also organized and performed in a variety show at Newton High School that benefited special-needs students.

As I fulfilled my practice teaching requirement in District 5, I was continually impressed by its high educational standards and its longstanding record of producing students whose SAT scores are among the highest in the nation. I would consider it a great opportunity to teach in such an accomplished district and hope to speak to you further about the available position.

Sincerely,

Chris Smith

Chris Smith

178 Green Street
Worcester, MA 01610
(508) 555-5555

June 23, 2001

Pat Cummings
Director
Any Agency
1140 Main Street
Salem, MA 01970

Dear Ms. Cummings:

Thank you for taking the time to speak with me today. As I mentioned on the phone, I am interested in beginning a career in the field of gerontology.

I am currently a senior at the College of the Holy Cross, majoring in Sociology. I have studied a variety of subjects, including gerontology, where I first became interested in this field. Other related courses I have taken include Poverty and Crisis, the Political Economy of Health Care in the United States, Race Relations, and Women in Society. My current grade point average is 3.64, and I am a member of the Phi Beta Kappa honor society.

In addition to my schoolwork, I am an active member of the student-run Volunteers for a Better World Program. Some of the experiences in which I have participated with this organization include serving Thanksgiving dinner to the homeless at a local soup kitchen, tutoring underprivileged junior high students in math and English, and codirecting a successful annual campus food drive. As a contributing writer for the *Angora,* I wrote many articles and editorials on social issues, including the plight of the elderly.

As a result of my classroom studies and my volunteer experience, I feel that I have a good grasp of the social and political issues that affect older adults in the United States, and I believe that at your agency. I could make a real difference in the lives of older people.

I've enclosed my resume and a sample article. Thank you for your attention, and I look forward to your response.

Sincerely,

Chris Smith

Chris Smith

RECENT GRADUATE
Legal Assistant

178 Green Street
Aston, PA 19014
(215) 555-5555

April 4, 2001

Pat Cummings
Attorney-at-Law
Any Firm
1140 Main Street
Erie, PA 16563

Dear Mr. Cummings:

Justice Ellen Malone, of the Allentown Courthouse, suggested that I contact you regarding an opening you may soon have for a legal assistant.

I will be graduating this May from Temple University with a Bachelor of Arts in African-American Studies. In addition to my core studies, I have studied in several areas, including business administration and computer applications. In 1998, I was awarded the prestigious Lieberman Scholarship.

I also offer a strong background in law, having worked in a variety of legal settings throughout my college years. I was a volunteer for Temple's Student Legal Aid, helping students with legal problems. I worked part-time over the past three years as a volunteer probation officer for the Allentown juvenile court. And in addition to being an outside media contact for an Aston Outreach Unified Neighborhood Team, I spent one summer as a research assistant for the Chief County Clerk of Allentown.

All these positions have given me a strong sense of the law and the American legal system. Moreover, this experience convinced me that I would like to pursue the law as a career. Justice Malone highly recommends your firm as one that might be a good match for my goals and qualifications.

I will contact you within the week to further discuss the possibility of securing this position. Thank you for your time.

Sincerely,

Chris Smith

Chris Smith

RECENT GRADUATE
Set Designer

178 Green Street
Columbia, SC 29202
(803) 555-5555

August 14, 2001

Pat Cummings
Stage Director
Any Production Company
1140 Main Street
Columbia, SC 29202

Dear Mr. Cummings:

Lynne Winchester recently indicated that you may have an opening for a set designer and suggested that I contact you. I am seeking a position involving stage design in television.

I graduated last December from Clemson University with a Bachelor of Arts degree in Theatre Arts and a concentration in Studio Art. In addition to modern drama and music and sound in theatre, I completed courses in set creation and design, intermediate painting, and woodworking. As a member of the drama club, I designed and helped create props for numerous campus productions, including *The Tempest* and *Marco Polo Sings a Solo.*

As for my work experience, I co-designed and co-created the props and decorations for a new miniature golf course with a tropical island theme, which turned out to be a big hit. I also gained valuable skills working as an apprentice to a busy carpenter and painting houses for a large company.

Enclosed is my resume as well as some photographs of my work. I have some great ideas for the sets of *Trivia Tunes* and *Videos after Dark* and hope to have the opportunity to discuss them with you.

Thank you for your consideration.

Sincerely,

Chris Smith

Chris Smith

RECENT GRADUATE
Translator

178 Green Street
Chicago Heights, IL 60411
(708) 555-5555

July 5, 2001

Pat Cummings
Director
Any Council
1140 Main Street
Denver, CO 80204

Dear Ms. Cummings:

I would like to apply for the position of translator advertised in the *Rocky Mountain News*.

I graduated last month with a Bachelor of Arts in International Relations and French Language from Northwestern University. Throughout my university career I was recognized for excellent scholarship, including being consistently on the Dean's list and graduating one year early, with honors and advanced standing. I was also active in many extracurricular events and organizations, including a residential honors program, in which I studied ethics and politics. By my junior year, I had become a Model United Nations Advisor, an alumni ambassador, and president of the International Affairs Society.

In addition, I have work experience in the field of international affairs, having been employed as an interpreter and translator for a Parisian film corporation. In this position, I interpreted for negotiations over film coproductions and translated agreements, film scripts, scenarios, and foreign correspondence. I also worked as the assistant to the Parisian correspondent for Desliases Associates, a prestigious import/export company.

I am not limited by location and would enjoy the opportunity to live and work in Denver for Any Council.

I look forward to hearing from you.

Sincerely,

Chris Smith

Chris Smith

TEMPORARY EMPLOYMENT HISTORY
Administrative Assistant

178 Green Street
Van Nuys, CA 91411
(818) 555-5555

October 1, 2001

Pat Cummings
Director
Any Temporary Agency
1140 Main Street
Van Nuys, CA 91411

Dear Ms. Cummings:

I am forwarding the enclosed resume for your consideration regarding suitable temporary assignment positions.

My five years of consecutive temporary assignment work have provided me with skills and qualifications applicable to many different fields. In short, I would offer a potential employer:

- Three years' accounting, financial, and administrative experience
- Computer knowledge, including PC and Macintosh
- Proficiency in word processing and spreadsheets
- Outstanding communication and organizational skills

I would prefer to receive an assignment in the Van Nuys area, and compensation requirements are negotiable. I look forward to hearing from you.

Sincerely,

Chris Smith

Chris Smith

178 Green Street
Scottsdale, AZ 85254
(602) 555-5555

May 13, 2001

Pat Cummings
Manager of Operations
Any Airport
1140 Main Street
Phoenix, AR 85021

Dear Ms. Cummings:

I am currently investigating opportunities to which I can apply my knowledge of, and extensive experience in, the management of large parking facilities.

In my most recent position at Parkinson Hotel, my abilities resulted in rapid advancement to a management position after only one year of service as a parking attendant. As supervisor of parking facilities, I oversaw all financial collections, maintained customer service standards, resolved problems, and managed a large staff. I also administered work schedules and payroll, assigned duties, and interfaced with hotel management.

I am a self-motivated, people-oriented, responsible individual, capable of meeting your expectations for quality supervision. I hope to have the opportunity to further discuss how I can contribute to your parking staff.

Sincerely,

Chris Smith

Chris Smith

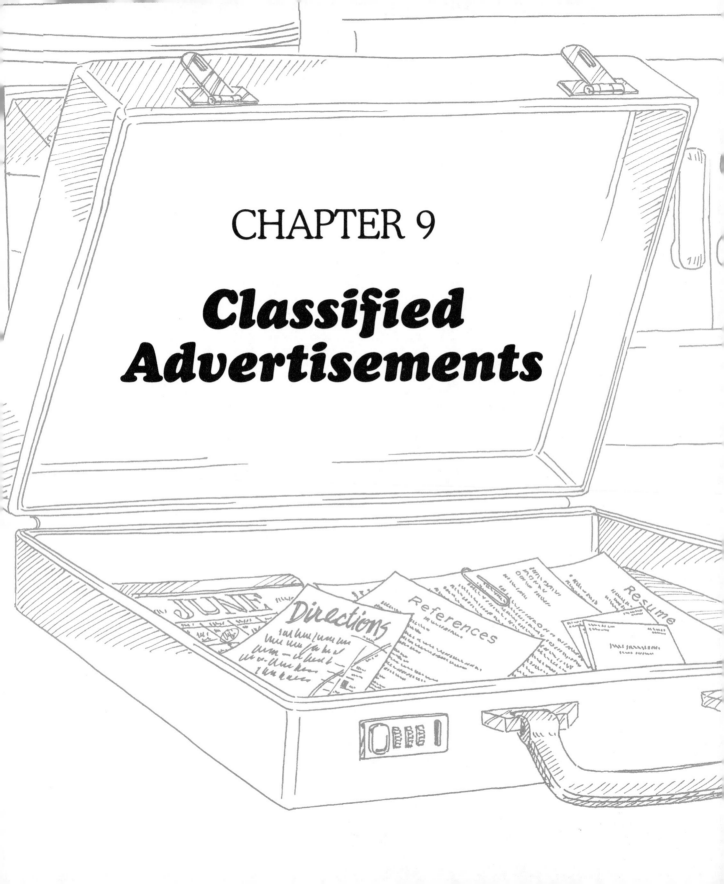

RESPONSE TO A CLASSIFIED ADVERTISEMENT
Administrative Assistant

178 Green Street
Ecru, MS 38842
(601) 555-5555

November 1, 2001

Pat Cummings
Office Manager
Any Corporation
1140 Main Street
Chicago, IL 60605

Dear Mr. Cummings:

Your advertisement in the *Jackson Review* calls for an assistant with a background in a variety of administrative skills, such as mine.

As an administrative assistant at Lambert Hospital, I was in charge of all computer support, word processing, and database, spreadsheet, and administrative functions. My duties included purchasing, equipment maintenance, daily office operations, supervising staff and volunteers, and coordinating various projects with staff and outside vendors.

I hope you will give me the opportunity to discuss the available position with you.

Sincerely,

Chris Smith

Chris Smith

RESPONSE TO A CLASSIFIED ADVERTISEMENT
Administrative Judge

178 Green Street
Fox, OR 97831
(503) 555-5555

June 6, 2001

Pat Cummings
Chairperson
Chicago Municipal Court
1140 Main Street
Chicago, IL 60605

Dear Ms. Cummings:

Your advertisement in the May 30th issue of *Lawyers Monthly* is of great interest to me. I feel that I have the qualifications necessary to effectively handle the responsibilities of Administrative Judge.

During the past four years as Assistant Attorney General, I have gained broad experience in the litigation of personal injury actions and workers' compensation claims. In this position, I made extensive use of my legal knowledge as well as my research, analytical, writing, and judgmental skills. I am confident of my ability to provide the expertise necessary for the professional representation of an Administrative Judge.

The enclosed resume describes my qualifications for the position advertised. I would welcome the opportunity to personally discuss my qualifications with you at your convenience.

Sincerely,

Chris Smith

Chris Smith
Enc. resume

178 Green Street
Henniker, NH 03242
(603) 555-5555

December 30, 2001

Pat Cummings
Director, Financial Planning
Any Corporation
1140 Main Street
Nashua, NH 03061

Dear Mr. Cummings:

I write in response to your advertisement for an Analyst in the December 28 edition of the *Telegraph*. During the past several years I have been actively involved, in both academic and workplace settings, with financial and business analysis as well as support activities involving corporate business and finance.

Although my present position has provided me with the opportunity for quality professional development as an Analyst and interesting challenges through diverse assignments, I am ready for a change. I am interested in joining a firm in which I can offer my analytical and qualitative skills toward making a substantial contribution to its overall success and reputation.

The enclosed employment profile is a summary of my experience. I would be glad to schedule an interview to discuss your requirements and my ability to handle the responsibilities of the position offered.

Should you require additional information prior to our meeting, please feel free to contact me at the above address and daytime number, or during the evenings at (603) 444-4444.

In the interim, I will look forward to your return response.

Yours sincerely,

Chris Smith

Chris Smith

RESPONSE TO A CLASSIFIED ADVERTISEMENT
Assistant Curator

178 Green Street
Bensonville, IL 60106
(708) 555-5555

June 21, 2001

Pat Cummings
Curator
Any Music Library
1140 Main Street
Evansville, IL 47713

Dear Ms. Cummings:

I wish to be considered for the position of Assistant Curator of your music library as advertised in last Friday's *Evansville Courier.*

My experience includes working as the Assistant Editor of *Classics Quarterly*, writing classical music reviews for the *Complete Record Guide*, conducting interviews and writing concert reviews for *Chicago Rock*, and writing rock and country album reviews for *Inside Edge*. I was also employed as the Classical Music Listings Coordinator for the *Complete Musical Almanac* summer and fall supplements. Currently, I am proofreading and copyediting part-time for *Art Illinois*, and am doing evening announcements (two nights per week) at WKEM in Belleville.

In addition, I offer a Bachelor of Arts in Music, a master's degree in Musicology from DePaul University, a year at Cambridge University (England) studying music and the arts, and doctoral studies at the University of Chicago.

I am very interested in resuming regular, full-time employment with a facility in need of a skilled professional knowledgeable in all aspects of musicology. I have often visited and relied on the resources available at Any Music Library, and would welcome the opportunity to join your ranks. I am confident my experience could be applied to a successful career as your Assistant Curator.

I would be happy to meet with you to further discuss the position and my ability to meet your needs. I will be in the Evansville area during the week of July 3, and will call your office to schedule a convenient interview time.

Thank you for your time.

Sincerely,

Chris Smith

Chris Smith

RESPONSE TO A CLASSIFIED ADVERTISEMENT
Assistant Editor

178 Green Street
Worcester, MA 01610
(508) 555-5555
csmith@netmail.com

June 28, 2001

Pat Cummings
Editor
Any Corporation
1140 Main Street
Boston, MA 02215

Dear Mr. Cummings:

I would like to apply for the position of assistant editor advertised in the *Boston Globe*. I possess strong written and verbal communication skills as well as computer and desktop publishing experience. My accomplishments include:

- Winning the Columbia Scholastic Press Association's First Place Gold Circle Award for graphic art
- Serving as features editor, art editor, graphic artist, and reporter for various college publications
- Completing a course in advertising art and desktop publishing, using Pagemaker
- Proficiency in WordPerfect and Lotus 1-2-3

I hope you will give me the opportunity to discuss the available position. Thank you for your consideration.

Sincerely,

Chris Smith

Chris Smith

RESPONSE TO A CLASSIFIED ADVERTISEMENT
Assistant Hospital Supervisor

178 Green Street
Stoughton, MA 02072
(617) 555-5555

July 27, 2001

Pat Cummings
Administrator
Any Corporation
1140 Main Street
Chicago, IL 60605

RE: Assistant Hospital Supervisor position

Dear Ms. Cummings:

I am writing in response to your advertisement in this past week's *Boston Phoenix*.

I recently took a sabbatical and finished my Bachelor of Arts in May at Emerson College. I am currently seeking full-time employment.

My employment background consists of twelve years at the Deaconess Hospital, where I provided a wide range of administrative, financial, and research support to the Chief Executive Officer. I have a strong aptitude for working with numbers and extensive experience with computer software applications.

I would be interested in speaking with you further regarding this position. I am hopeful that you will consider my background in administrative support, as well as my word processing, data base, and spreadsheet skills an asset to Any Corporation.

Thank you in advance for your consideration.

Sincerely,

Chris Smith

Chris Smith

Enc. resume

RESPONSE TO A CLASSIFIED ADVERTISEMENT
Associate Desktop Publisher

178 Green Street
Tacoma, WA 98447
(206) 555-5555
csmith@netmail.com

March 10, 2001

Pat Cummings
Managing Editor
Any Corporation
1140 Main Street
Richmond, VA 23225

Dear Mr. Cummings:

In response to your advertisement for an Associate Desktop Publisher, I am sending my resume for your review.

My ten years of computer experience include researching, developing, and documenting the operational procedures of a software seller. I was responsible for all aspects of the manual, from conceptualization to publication. I also coordinated and published the sales and marketing of a newsletter distributed to key accounts and sales representatives.

Successful completion of such projects requires skills in researching, organizing, writing, and editing. I am proficient in several desktop publishing and word processing applications, including WordPerfect, Microsoft Word, and Corel Ventura.

I will be moving to the Richmond area next week and would be happy to meet with you at your convenience. I will call your office during the week of March 17. Thank you.

Sincerely,

Chris Smith

Chris Smith
Enc. resume

RESPONSE TO A CLASSIFIED ADVERTISEMENT
Athletic Director

178 Green Street
La Crosse, WI 54601
(608) 555-5555

September 23, 2001

Pat Cummings
Headmaster
Any School
1140 Main Street
Brownsville, TX 78520

Dear Ms. Cummings:

I am writing to you regarding the opening for the position of Athletic Director, as advertised in the *Wisconsin State Journal*. I believe that, with my background in athletics and science, I have the technical knowledge, work ethic, and organizational skills to contribute to your team.

For the past nine years I have been coaching rowing. I feel strongly that the qualities embodied in rowing have made me successful in my various business and athletic endeavors. Goal setting, discipline, determination, and teamwork are applicable to any field.

I admire Any School's unique educational philosophy, which stresses the utility of athletics to instill discipline in young minds. I feel that I can contribute to your school's achievement-oriented environment.

Due to a change in the position of Head Crew Coach at Yale University, I was put in an interim position of responsibility for the smooth running of the boathouse. For the 2000-2001 season, I dealt with all the ordering, budgeting, donation solicitation, spare parts inventory, and travel arrangements for the crews. I was, in effect, the administrative head of the boathouse.

I will call in approximately two weeks to discuss how I hope to contribute to your school. A resume is enclosed for your consideration.

Sincerely,

Chris Smith

Chris Smith

RESPONSE TO A CLASSIFIED ADVERTISEMENT
Business Consultant

178 Green Street
Payne Gap, KY 41537
(606) 555-5555
csmith@netmail.com

June 3, 2001

Pat Cummings
Director of Recruiting
Any Corporation
1140 Main Street
Payne Gap, KY 41537

Dear Mr. Cummings:

I am a new MBA graduate from Spain's premiere business school, la Universidad de Negocios. Although I have lived in Spain for most of my life, I am an American citizen and have just recently moved to Kentucky to seek permanent employment.

Your advertisement in the *Lexington Herald-Leader* captured my attention because I am very interested in pursuing a career as a software consultant. Please allow me to highlight my qualifications as they relate to your stated requirements.

Your Requirements
- Experience consulting to small businesses
- Experience working in small businesses
- Marketing experience
- Enjoy using computers

My Experience
- Graduated with an M.B.A. Immersed in case study method, in which students act as consultants, analyzing and solving business problems.
- Founded Widgetsoft, a software development business.
- 4-1/2 years of progressive marketing experience.
- Fluency in Lotus 1-2-3, Microsoft Word, Word for Windows, dBase. Programming experience in C+, Fortran, COBOL.

I believe my qualifications are commensurate with your requirements for this position.

Sincerely,

Chris Smith

Chris Smith

RESPONSE TO A CLASSIFIED ADVERTISEMENT
Campus Police Officer

178 Green Street
Stanford, CA 94305
(415) 555-5555

February 23, 2001

Pat Cummings
Director of Security
Any College
1140 Main Street
Whittier, CA 92608

RE: Campus Police Officer

Dear Ms. Cummings:

My interest in pursuing and expanding my professional career in law enforcement and security management has prompted me to respond to your advertisement in the March issue of *Careers in Law Enforcement.*

For the past twelve years, my background has been concentrated in security and law enforcement. In my present position, I am responsible for maintaining the highest possible site and operations security for a key United States government defense contractor. From 1987 to 1995, I served in the United States Army where I was responsible for maintaining peak law enforcement/security alertness and the welfare of all personnel. In that capacity, I received numerous letters of commendation for superior job performance. I am a graduate of military police school, I have completed additional law enforcement seminars, and I am enrolled in a criminal justice program.

Through practical experience, I am well versed in military and international law as well as United States law and procedures. If we could meet in a personal interview, I could discuss further my qualifications and outline the potential contribution I could make to your security office.

I look forward to your response.

Sincerely,

Chris Smith

Chris Smith

RESPONSE TO A CLASSIFIED ADVERTISEMENT
Canine Science Instructor

178 Green Street
Winesburg, OH 44690
(614) 555-5555

February 25, 2001

Pat Cummings
Academic Administrator
Any College
1140 Main Street
Cincinnati, OH 45202

RE: Canine Science Instructor

Dear Mr. Cummings:

My interest in the position of part-time Instructor for courses in animal grooming and behavior training advertised in the February 24 edition of the *Cincinnati Post* has prompted me to forward my resume for your review.

In addition to a Bachelor of Arts in Behavioral Sciences, I hold certificates in Kennel Management, Dog Grooming, Training, and continue to attend seminars in adult dog and puppy training. Beyond my academic pursuits, I have more than six years of hands-on experience teaching group obedience classes for dogs and puppies. I also provide private lessons, behavioral consultations, and training for AKC Titles.

After you have had the opportunity to review my qualifications, I would appreciate meeting with you to further discuss this position. I am well qualified to teach future instructors in courses on animal grooming and behavior training, and feel confident that I can provide the kind of student support expected by Any College.

Yours sincerely,

Chris Smith

Chris Smith

RESPONSE TO A CLASSIFIED ADVERTISEMENT
Case Manager

178 Green Street
White Plains, NY 10606
(914) 555-5555

December 17, 2001

Pat Cummings
Director of Social Services
Any Agency
1140 Main Street
Hoboken, NJ 07030

Dear Ms. Cummings:

I am responding to your advertisement in the *Star Ledger* in search of a Case Manager. My interest is in pursuing and expanding my professional career in the motivation and guidance of juveniles to achieve positive objectives and personal dignity. It is this goal that has prompted me to forward the attached resume for your review and consideration.

Please note that I have directed and dedicated my efforts, both academically and through the co-op program at Fordham University, to working with juveniles and prison inmates, guiding them through innovative programs in self-preservation. These programs required extensive communication and interaction with boards of trustees, agency personnel, and the Neighborhood Watch campaign. In addition, I have acquired excellent customer/client relations and communications skills, as well as sound knowledge of office procedures, in a variety of full-time and part-time positions.

I would welcome a meeting to learn more about your work at Any Agency and how I could contribute to your success.

Yours sincerely,

Chris Smith

Chris Smith

RESPONSE TO A CLASSIFIED ADVERTISEMENT
Chief Financial Officer

178 Green Street
Rigby, ID 83442

June 25, 2001

Pat Cummings
Controller
Any Corporation
1140 Main Street
Boise, ID 83706

RE: Chief Financial Officer

Dear Mr. Cummings:

With reference to the above-advertised position, the attached resume is submitted for your evaluation.

I have a record of outstanding success in the management of corporate financial operations for fast-paced manufacturing companies and associated commercial operations in multi-location, multistate, and international environments.

My sixteen years of progressively responsible experience encompassed management of all aspects of the financial and treasury functions, in a range from Cost Accounting Manager to Chief Financial Officer and Vice-President, Finance. This experience has encompassed the successful management of corporate real estate, human resources, and general operations. In addition to holding a M.B.A. in Finance and a Bachelor of Arts in Accounting, I have been a Certified Public Accountant since 1983.

Please contact me at the above address or call (208) 555-5555 (home) or (208) 444-4444 (office), as I would like to arrange a mutually convenient time for a meeting, during which we can further discuss your current or anticipated openings. May I hear from you?

Yours sincerely,

Chris Smith

Chris Smith

RESPONSE TO A CLASSIFIED ADVERTISEMENT
Child Care Director

178 Green Street
Lima, OH 45804
(419) 555-5555

July 18, 2001

Pat Cummings
Director
Any Center
1140 Main Street
Toledo, OH 43660

Dear Ms. Cummings:

I am responding to your advertisement for an assistant center director in the *Toledo Blade*.

I am a licensed child care provider in the state of Ohio with three years' experience working in a private center, facilitating the care of over forty children. In this capacity, I have been solely responsible for supervising ten children, ranging in age from six months to five years. My duties include distributing meals and snacks, monitoring playtime, and creating, and instructing children in, diverse educational activities.

I also have experience working with children in other settings, having held positions such as private nanny, tutor, camp counselor, and gymnastics instructor. I am the author of a children's book, *Home We Go!*

I would appreciate the opportunity to speak to you further about this position.

With best regards,

Chris Smith

Chris Smith

RESPONSE TO A CLASSIFIED ADVERTISEMENT
Claims Adjuster

178 Green Street
Salisbury, NC 28145
(704) 555-5555

August 26, 2001

Pat Cummings
Claims Supervisor
Any Insurance Agency
1140 Main Street
Asheville, NC 28802

Dear Mr. Cummings:

I would like to apply for the claims adjuster position advertised in the *Citizen Times*. During the past fifteen years, I have been employed by a major insurance company, where my primary area of concentration has been in handling workers' compensation claims.

Due to my company's consolidation, I am currently seeking an organization in need of a highly productive individual with a sound background in claims handling, cost containment, customer relations/service, employee training, and administrative support. I have cost-effectively negotiated over one hundred claims in a six-month period.

I am well organized, am capable of researching and coordinating detailed data, and can work effectively with professionals and corporate management to arrive at mutually favorable solutions.

I hope you will give me the opportunity speak to you about applying my skills to your organization.

Sincerely,

Chris Smith

Chris Smith

RESPONSE TO A CLASSIFIED ADVERTISEMENT
Clinical Research Nurse

178 Green Street
Marietta, GA 30060
(404) 555-5555

August 20, 2001

Pat Cummings, R.N.
Head Nurse
Any Hospital
1140 Main Street
Savannah, GA 31404

Dear Ms. Cummings:

I would like to apply for the clinical research nurse opening advertised in *Nursing Today*.

I am a dedicated professional capable of working with physicians and nursing, laboratory, and professional specialty groups. I have a Bachelor of Science in Nursing and more than fourteen years of responsible experience, ranging from staff nurse and charge nurse to clinical research nurse with a major teaching hospital. My graduate studies have focused on epidemiology and international health. My experience encompasses sound knowledge of nursing quality assurance programs and in-service education programs. Throughout my career, I have worked on studies involving psoriasis, cardiology, AIDS, sickle-cell anemia, amyloid, diabetes, and oncology.

I hope to speak with you soon. Thank you for your consideration.

Sincerely,

Chris Smith

Chris Smith, R.N., B.S.N.

RESPONSE TO A CLASSIFIED ADVERTISEMENT
Conference Coordinator

178 Green Street
Racine, WI 53406

December 22, 2001

Pat Cummings
Artistic Director
Any Deaf Theatre
1140 Main Street
De Forest, WI 53532

Dear Mr. Cummings:

The position of Conference Director advertised the January issue of *Deaf Today* is of great interest of me, and I have enclosed my resume for your review.

I am a deaf person who has had the opportunity to complete my undergraduate and graduate studies, and who has worked in responsible positions requiring strong leadership, planning, organizational, administrative, and communication skills. Throughout my career, I have worked with individuals and groups in diverse settings within public, private, artistic, and government sectors.

I am well versed in visual and performing arts as a student, performer, coordinator, instructor, and facilitator with concentration in providing services for, and instructing, the deaf community and the general public. I have the communication, public relations, and people skills to establish an annual conference for Any Deaf Theatre that will meet the criteria of excellence you are looking for in a lasting international artistic exchange. It is a challenging undertaking that I feel I am capable of achieving.

Should you need additional information, please contact me at (414) 555-5555 TTY or at csmith@netmail.com.

I look forward to your return response.

Sincerely,

Chris Smith

Chris Smith

RESPONSE TO A CLASSIFIED ADVERTISEMENT
Contracted Typist

178 Green Street
Baltimore, MD 21202
(301) 555-5555

February 14, 2001

Pat Cummings
Sales Manager
Any Corporation
1140 Main Street
Washington, DC 19180

Dear Ms. Cummings:

I would like to apply for the contract typist position advertised in the *Washington Post*.

My qualifications for this position include a typing speed of 70 wpm on an IBM Selectric typewriter and 90 wpm on a computer keyboard. I hold an Associate of Arts in English from Newbury Junior College. I have a PC with a laser printer and, for word processing, Word and WordPerfect.

I look forward to hearing from you.

With best regards,

Chris Smith

Chris Smith

RESPONSE TO A CLASSIFIED ADVERTISEMENT
Cosmetologist

178 Green Street
Auburn, WA 98071
(206) 555-5555

August 13, 2001

Pat Cummings
Owner
Any Boutique
1140 Main Street
Seattle, WA 98134

Dear Mr. Cummings:

    Enclosed please find my resume. I am very interested in applying for the position of Cosmetologist that was advertised in the *Seattle Post Intelligencer* on August 13, and am confident that you will find my skills ideally applicable to your needs.

    Thank you in advance for your anticipated consideration. I look forward to meeting with you to discuss this opportunity.

Sincerely,

Chris Smith

Chris Smith

RESPONSE TO A CLASSIFIED ADVERTISEMENT
Customer Service Representative

178 Green Street
Decorah, IA 51201
(319) 555-5555

September 6, 2001

Pat Cummings
Director of Public Relations
Any Corporation
1140 Main Street
Northampton, MA 01060

Dear Ms. Cummings:

I would like to apply for the customer service support position advertised in the *Sunday Globe*.

During the past several years at Fortmiller, Inc., my experience has been in the areas of billing, credit, collection, and customer service. In my current position as customer service supervisor, I maintain the efficiency and accuracy of complex billing systems. This position also requires generating detailed reports for management. My position has given me the opportunity to set policies and procedures, implement systems, and participate in staffing and training personnel. During my tenure, 55 percent of the entry-level staff I trained advanced to managerial positions within Fortmiller. I am confident of my ability to provide you with the experience and quality of performance you expect.

I look forward to hearing from you.

Sincerely,

Chris Smith

Chris Smith

RESPONSE TO A CLASSIFIED ADVERTISEMENT
Dental Hygienist

178 Green Street
Deer Park, NY 11729
(516) 555-5555

March 3, 2001

Pat Cummings
Dentist
1140 Main Street
Lynbrook, NY 11563

Dear Mr. Cummings:

I would like to offer the attached confidential resume as an application for the Dental Hygienist position you advertised in the *Times-Union*.

I am confident that my training and experience could be effectively applied to the requirements of the position as described. If you would like any additional information, please do not hesitate to contact me. I look forward to meeting with you and further discussing the mutual benefit of our joining forces.

Thank you in advance for your consideration.

Sincerely,

Chris Smith

Chris Smith
Enc. resume

RESPONSE TO A CLASSIFIED ADVERTISEMENT
Dentistry Department Manager

178 Green Street
Gaithersburg, MD 20879

February 10, 2001

Pat Cummings
Chief Administrator
Any Hospital
1140 Main Street
Chapel Hill, NC 27514

RE: Manager—Department of Dentistry

Dear Ms. Cummings:

The position you advertised is of great interest to me, and I hope to convince you of my capability to cost-effectively execute the responsibilities of Dentistry Department Manager.

My experience with Johns Hopkins Medical School's Department of Ophthalmology, Maryland Eye & Ear Infirmary, and Blue Cross/Blue Shield has involved interfacing and dealing with all operations and administrative departments on matters pertaining to fiscal and business reporting. I have extensive experience with MIS and firsthand experience with sophisticated programs designed to accommodate and control the rapid and profitable growth of business.

My business management, staff training and supervision, and administrative experience are essential requirements for maintaining equitable controls for a highly complex business. I can provide cost-effective fiscal management to maintain and increase profitability. Through efficient tracking and control systems, budget planning, and administration, I can generate cost savings and greater profit margins.

Should you require additional information, I will be glad to meet with you for further discussion. I can be reached at (301) 555-5555. In the interim, I look forward to meeting with you and joining your management team in the near future.

Sincerely,

Chris Smith

Chris Smith
Enc. resume

RESPONSE TO A CLASSIFIED ADVERTISEMENT
Director of Public Works

178 Green Street
Liberty, SC 29657
(803) 555-5555

September 22, 2001

Pat Cummings
District Supervisor
Any Office
1140 Main Street
Charleston, SC 29403

Dear Mr. Cummings:

I am very interested in the position of Director of Public Works for the town of Liberty as advertised in the September 20 edition of the *Post and Courier.*

During the past thirteen years, I have been actively involved in the management of diverse projects which require the ability to work with engineering, architectural, and construction professionals on public and private rehabilitation, restoration, and construction programs. My experience ranges from concept to sign-off and the supervision of in-house and field crews on both privately and city/federally funded building and highway contracts.

I am an effective manager and budget administrator, and have the ability to work in harmony with individuals and groups in a busy construction/public works environment where concentration is on community services, safety, and the environment. As a longtime resident in the town of Liberty, I believe I could reflect personal, as well as the local interest in providing quality DPW services. I am confident of my ability to direct an efficient, cost-effective, and productive department.

Enclosed is my business profile for your consideration. I would like to learn more about the position, and will call your office early next week to see if we can schedule a meeting.

Thank you for your time.

Sincerely,

Chris Smith

Chris Smith

RESPONSE TO A CLASSIFIED ADVERTISEMENT
Editorial Assistant

178 Green Street
Austin, TX 78746
(512) 555-5555
csmith@netmail.com

June 4, 2001

Pat Cummings
Vice-President
Any Corporation
1140 Main Street
Dallas, TX 75275

Dear Ms. Cummings:

I am very interested in the Editorial Assistant position listed recently in the *Dallas Morning News*, and am including my resume and a writing sample as an application. I am familiar with Any Corporation's publications, and would love the opportunity to contribute to your efforts.

My accomplishments include:

- Experience editing books and other materials for a wide variety of clients, including Reiling Press, Wilson Smith, and numerous corporate clients.
- Experience writing consumer materials, including chapters for fiction books published by Hollis Press, and a complete nonfiction book entitled *Easy Do It Resumes* (O'Leary Press).

Should you need additional information or writing samples, please feel free to contact me at the above-listed number. I look forward to joining the editorial team at Any Corporation, and will call your office next week to discuss this opportunity further.

Thank you.

Sincerely,

Chris Smith

Chris Smith

RESPONSE TO A CLASSIFIED ADVERTISEMENT
Events Planner

178 Green Street
Tiverton, RI 02878
(401) 555-5555

August 21, 2001

Pat Cummings
Vice-President of Public Relations
Any Corporation
1140 Main Street
Chicago, IL 60605

Dear Mr. Cummings:

Please accept this letter as an application for the Events Planner position advertised in the *Providence Journal* on August 20. My confidential resume is enclosed for your review.

The position described is exactly the opportunity I am looking for. I am confident my six years' experience in public relations, coupled with my drive and enthusiasm, would enable me to make a significant contribution to your organization.

I believe the most important qualification of an Events Planner is the ability to plan well and soundly, and then to imbue a staff with the spirit of teamwork—in other words, to provide leadership and effective administration. I would describe myself as a well-organized, results-oriented, and effective problem-solver.

I welcome the opportunity to meet with you to further discuss my qualifications and your needs. Thank you for your time and consideration.

Sincerely,

Chris Smith

Chris Smith
Enc. resume

RESPONSE TO A CLASSIFIED ADVERTISEMENT
Features Reporter

178 Green Street
Emmitsburg, MD 21727
(301) 555-5555
csmith@netmail.com

July 20, 2001

Pat Cummings
Senior Reporter
Any Newspaper
1140 Main Street
Largo, MD 20772

Dear Ms. Cummings:

I would like to apply for the features reporter position advertised in the *Baltimore Sun*.

As you will note from the enclosed resume, I have experience in various areas of journalism. My internship with the *Emmitsburg News* provided me the opportunity to sharpen my researching skills. My duties included field reporting, writing copy, and editing a variety of articles. My skills in photography enabled me to provide photos to accompany stories. In addition, while completing my degree at Mount St. Mary's, I worked as editor of the yearbook and layout editor of the student newspaper, where I became proficient in desktop publishing.

I look forward to hearing from you.

Sincerely,

Chris Smith

Chris Smith

RESPONSE TO A CLASSIFIED ADVERTISEMENT
Field Finance Manager

178 Green Street
Richmond, VA 23220

January 17, 2001

Pat Cummings
Chief Financial Officer
Any Corporation
1140 Main Street
Washington, DC 20002

Dear Mr. Cummings:

I am inquiring about the Central Area Field Finance Manager position advertised in the
Richmond Times-Dispatch.

Enclosed you will find my resume, which details the skills necessary to enhance the central
area's performance:

- Experience advising Fortune 100 and small company senior management on
  strategy, planning, and budgeting.
- Strong accounting and finance academic preparation combined with significant work
  experience.
- Excellent working knowledge of microcomputer technology.

Please feel free to contact me at (804) 555-5555 if you have any questions and would like
to meet.

Sincerely yours,

Chris Smith

Chris Smith

RESPONSE TO A CLASSIFIED ADVERTISEMENT
Film Archivist

178 Green Street
New Castle, DE 19270
(302) 555-5555

July 22, 2001

Pat Cummings
Curator
Any Library
1140 Main Street
Macon, GA 31201

RE: Film Archivist Position; *Moving Picture Pictorial*, July 19, 2001

Dear Ms. Cummings:

I am interested in your advertised position for a Film Archivist. My passion for film and my applicable skills make me confident that I am a qualified candidate.

Currently, I am a reporter for the *Vertov Film Journal*, a monthly entertainment magazine. In addition, I am capable of shooting, printing, and developing 35-mm, black-and-white film. During my last year at Brandeis, I researched, wrote, and edited a one-hundred page senior honors thesis on the filmmaker Sergei Eisenstein. I enjoyed that project immensely, and would enjoy researching film and film-related literature on a daily basis.

I am aware that your library's film archive is the largest in the South. I would welcome the opportunity to employ my talents at Any Library, and am willing to relocate if offered the position.

I have enclosed a resume and a few writing samples for you to look over at your convenience. Thank you for your time, and I hope to meet with you soon to discuss your Film Archivist position even further.

Sincerely,

Chris Smith

Chris Smith

RESPONSE TO A CLASSIFIED ADVERTISEMENT
Fundraiser

178 Green Street
Roswell, NM 88202

June 2, 2001

Pat Cummings
Director
Any Organization
1140 Main Street
Alamogordo, NM 88311

Dear Mr. Cummings:

I am writing in response to your advertisement for a fundraiser that appears in this month's *Not-for-Profit Now!* Your organization strikes me as particularly dynamic, and I know that my energy, enthusiasm, and skills can only complement the success of your fiscal campaigns.

After graduating from the University of New Mexico last June, I have been working in the University's development office at the Office of Public Programs. UNM is in its second year of a $450 million capital campaign—$25 million of which was achieved this fall in a single record-breaking donation. My role in this stimulating and exciting time at the University has been as the Campaign Registration Coordinator. This position has afforded me many valuable experiences, not the least of which has been working for the University's expert fundraisers. Observant to detail and acutely aware of my surroundings, I have had the opportunity to become appreciative of the techniques of my colleagues, responsive to the interests of a variety of personalities, and proactive in the fulfillment of our goals. My job demands efficiency, precision, and the ability to juggle several different projects simultaneously. I feel confident that I can apply my skills in your organization.

Capable and eager, I am seeking this challenge. I have enclosed my resume for your consideration. I look forward to speaking with you soon about my qualifications, and can be reached easily at (505) 555-5555.

Sincerely,

Chris Smith

Chris Smith

RESPONSE TO A CLASSIFIED ADVERTISEMENT
Gemologist

178 Green Street
Gainseville, FL 36608
(904) 555-5555

June 2, 2001

Pat Cummings
Vice-President
Any Institute
1140 Main Street
Tampa, FL 33611

Dear Ms. Cummings:

I was very excited to read about the opening for a Gemologist in the latest edition of your company newsletter. I would like to submit my credentials as an application for this opportunity.

I became interested in the import/export of precious gems several years ago while living in Nepal. Upon my return to the United States, I enrolled in what my research revealed to be the best gemology school, the Gemologist Institute of America, in Santa Monica, California. This year I graduated with honors, and hold the title of Graduate Gemologist.

The enclosed resume summarizes my background, most of which has an emphasis in public relations, sales, promotions, and dealing with people of all socioeconomic levels and cultures. I am presently searching for an opportunity, with an institute such as yours, which could benefit from my training, skills, and knowledge in the technical and business facets of gemology.

After you have reviewed my qualifications, I would appreciate interviewing with you for this position. I am very interested in the opportunity that it provides and am confident that my training and experience fit your requirements. Please note that I plan to follow up with a call in a few days.

Sincerely,

Chris Smith

Chris Smith

RESPONSE TO A CLASSIFIED ADVERTISEMENT
Home Economist/Coordinator

178 Green Street
Reno, NV 89520
(702) 555-5555

July 25, 2001

Pat Cummings
Director, Home Economics Program
Any University
1140 Main Street
Seattle, WA 98109

Dear Mr. Cummings:

My interest in the position of Home Economist/Coordinator described in your advertisement in the *Seattle Times* has prompted me to forward the attached resume for your evaluation.

In addition to earning a B.S. in Home Economics and Nutrition Education, I have completed coursework in psychology and learning development, and have undergone supplemental training at the professional level with each employer since graduation, including a teaching hospital.

I possess excellent verbal, written, and interpersonal skills. In addition, I hold extensive experience with the development and training-related duties of seminars in my areas of expertise, and relate easily to all age groups and socioeconomic levels. As an alumnus of the University of Washington at Seattle and a native of the state of Washington, I am well acquainted with the overall family/business environment in which I would be working.

I will be in Washington on Friday, August 5. I would like to arrange to meet with you at this time to convince you of my ability to successfully fill your position. I will call your office on July 27 to schedule an interview time.

Thank you very much for your consideration.

Sincerely,

Chris Smith

Chris Smith

RESPONSE TO A CLASSIFIED ADVERTISEMENT
Hospital Administor

178 Green Street
Lapeer, MI 48446
(313) 555-5555
cmith@netmail.com

June 17, 2001

Pat Cummings
District Vice-President
Any Health Resource Corporation
1140 Main Street
Flint, MI 48502

RE: Hospital Administrator

Dear Ms. Cummings:

After reading your advertisement in the *Flint Journal*, I believe that Keller Memorial Hospital is in need of an Administrator who can provide direction, as well as strong marketing and financial expertise, to develop and implement its purpose.

During my sixteen years as President/Treasurer of a multibranch, multistate prosthetics, orthodontics, DME business, I directed all phases of operations from the construction of headquarter and manufacturing facilities to the sales and marketing of custom and durable medical products. Also, I have a strong background in the preparation of business plans and strategies, financial and budget analysis, financial package design, and forecasts and projections. All of my motivation has been directed toward new business development and expanding services in the health care field.

In addition, I am a strong organizer, enthusiastic speaker, capable leader, and team player who can interface effectively with medical professionals as well as support staff. In the role of Hospital Director, I am confident that I can provide you with the energy and experience to achieve results, and would welcome the opportunity to reiterate this in a personal interview. I will contact your office next Monday to schedule a mutually covenient time to meet.

Thank you for your time.

Sincerely,

Chris Smith

Chris Smith

RESPONSE TO A CLASSIFIED ADVERTISEMENT
Hotel Manager

178 Green Street
Traverse City, MI 49684
(313) 555-5555

January 23, 2001

Pat Cummings
District Manager
Any Corporation
1140 Main Street
Marquette, MI 49855

Dear Mr. Cummings:

I would like to apply for the position of hotel manager advertised in the *Detroit Free Press*.

My experience in the hospitality industry is broad-based, and my accomplishments reflect a proven ability to perform in diverse and varied functions. My positions have ranged from front desk clerk and director of sales and marketing to my current position as assistant general manager of a prestigious three-thousand-room hotel. In this capacity I am responsible for all operation aspects of the rooms division, including front office, housekeeping, maintenance, reservations, quality control, and communications. I am also a member of the executive committee involved in all budgetary and policy decision-making.

I have been involved in hospitality management for ten years, and while my present position is satisfying, the position of hotel manager you offer seems to provide the ideal next step and an opportunity for a long-term association with a new organization. I would appreciate the opportunity to discuss your requirements and how I might fulfill them.

Thank you for your consideration.

Sincerely,

Chris Smith

Chris Smith

RESPONSE TO A CLASSIFIED ADVERTISEMENT
International Buyer

178 Green Street
Knoke, IA 50553
(515) 555-5555

February 3, 2001

Pat Cummings
Senior Marketing Manager
Any Corporation
1140 Main Street
Chicago, IL 60605

Dear Ms. Cummings:

In response to your advertisement in the February 1 edition of the *Chicago Sun-Times* for an International Buyer, I would like to submit my application for your consideration.

As you can see, my qualifications match those you seek:

You Require:
- A college degree
- Fluency in Italian and French
- Office experience
- Typing skills
- Willingness to travel

I Offer:
- A bachelor's degree in English from Long Island University
- Fluency in Italian, German, and French
- Experience as a receptionist at a busy accounting firm
- Accurate typing at 60 wpm
- A willingness to travel

I feel that I am well qualified for this position and can make a lasting contribution to Any Corporation.

I would welcome the opportunity for a personal interview with you at your convenience.

Sincerely,

Chris Smith

Chris Smith

RESPONSE TO A CLASSIFIED ADVERTISEMENT
Legal Assistant

178 Green Street
Shoshoni, WY 82649
(307) 555-5555

September 18, 2001

Pat Cummings
Partner
Any Corporation
1140 Main Street
Chicago, IL 60605

Dear Mr. Cummings:

I am writing in response to your advertisement for a legal assistant in the *New York Times.* Having recently graduated from the New England School of Law, I intend to relocate to Chicago.

My work experience and my scholastic endeavors have prepared me for employment in a firm that specializes in general practice. This fall and past summer, I have interned for a small general practice firm, where I am entrusted with a great deal of responsibility. I write appellate briefs, compose memoranda in corporate, contract, and criminal law, and draft complaints and answers. I also actively participate in attorney-client conferences by questioning clients and by describing how the law affects the clients' suits.

I would appreciate the opportunity to meet with you and discuss how my qualifications could meet your needs. Thank you for your consideration.

With best regards,

Chris Smith

Chris Smith, Esq.

RESPONSE TO A CLASSIFIED ADVERTISEMENT
Libraian

178 Green Street
Stanford, CA 94305
(415) 555-5555

January 24, 2001

Pat Cummings
Head Librarian
Any Library
1140 Main Street
Havre, MT 59501

Dear Ms. Cummings:

I was very excited to discover the availability of the Librarian position with Any Library. The job description as printed in the *Billings Gazette* suggests an "on-your-feet-and-running"-styled position, which would be a welcome extension of my present work.

My experience at the Stanford Law School for the past two years has focused mostly on editorial, research, and administrative work with book manuscripts, journals, and dissertations. I am confident this experience qualifies me for the position.

With that in mind, I enclose my resume and appreciate your consideration of me as a serious candidate. I am moving to Montana permanently next month, but would be happy to meet with you earlier for a personal interview.

Sincerely,

Chris Smith

Chris Smith

RESPONSE TO A CLASSIFIED ADVERTISEMENT
Loan Officer

178 Green Street
Owensboro, KY 42302

March 2, 2001

Pat Cummings, Branch Manager
Any Bank
1140 Main Street
Lexington, KY 40506

Dear Mr. Cummings:

In response to last Friday's advertisement in the *Lexington Herald-Leader* for a loan officer, I have enclosed my resume for your review. As you can see, my qualifications are an ideal match for your requirements.

You require:
- Over five years' experience.
- Skill in personnel and customer service relations.
- Extensive lending knowledge.
- A willingness to travel.

I offer:
- Nine years of rapidly progressive and responsible experience.
- Five years of full responsibility for the management of branch banking operations, training and directing, and for quality customer service and satisfaction.
- Skill in implementing institution policies, procedures, and practices concerning lending and new business development, and granting or extending lines of credit and commercial, real estate, and consumer loans.
- A willingness to travel.

Thank you for your consideration. I look forward to speaking with you.

Sincerely,

Chris Smith

Chris Smith

RESPONSE TO A CLASSIFIED ADVERTISEMENT
Masonry Supply Manager

178 Green Street
Waterbury, CT 06708

December 5, 2001

Pat Cummings
General Manager
Any Corporation
1140 Main Street
Hartford, CT 06115

Dear Ms. Cummings:

My interest in the position of Masonry Supply Manager (*Hartford Courant*, November 30) has prompted me to forward my resume.

During the past ten years, my experience has been concentrated in the masonry and plastering products supply industry with a building materials firm. During my six years as General Manager, I took an old line business, which had undergone several years of poor management, and reversed the trend. I upgraded the firm's image and customer and vendor relations, which subsequently increased the dollar volume and bottom line profits by 300 percent.

I will contact you in a few days to arrange a meeting for further discussion. In the interim, should you require additional information, I may be reached at (203) 555-5555 between 9:00 a.m. and 5:00 p.m.

Sincerely,

Chris Smith

Chris Smith

RESPONSE TO A CLASSIFIED ADVERTISEMENT
Meeting Planner

178 Green Street
Rohnert Park, CA 94928
(707) 555-5555

May 11, 2001

Pat Cummings
Vice-President, Marketing
Any Corporation
1140 Main Street
San Francisco, CA 94132

Dear Mr. Cummings:

After reading your advertisement in the *San Francisco Chronicle,* I believe my qualifications match your requirements for a meeting planner.

During the past seven years, I have held positions requiring communications, sales, marketing, and supervisory skills in people-oriented, retailing, media, and educational environments. I am a quick study and have good presentation and communications training. I can readily take direction and can provide organization, creative input, and an enthusiastic approach.

I hope you will give me the opportunity to speak to you about this position.

I appreciate your consideration.

Sincerely,

Chris Smith

Chris Smith

RESPONSE TO A CLASSIFIED ADVERTISEMENT
Multimedia Specialist

178 Green Street
Sparkill, NY 10976
(914) 555-5555
csmith@netmail.com

April 18, 2001

Pat Cummings
Director, Human Resources
Any Corporation
1140 Main Street
Staten Island, NY 10301

Dear Ms. Cummings:

This is in reply to your advertisement for a Multimedia Specialist published in the April 16 edition of the *New York Daily News*.

I have composed the following comparison demonstrating how my background and experience directly qualify me for the requirements listed for the position.

Your requirements:
- Lots of experience working in and consulting to small businesses.
- Enjoy using computers (but don't necessarily have any programming experience).
- Responsible for working with business writers, editors, and programmers to help design software packages for small businesses.

My qualifications:
- Generated over 50 percent of my consulting income in the past year from small business clients.
- Conceived of and authored an OS/2 Tips and Techniques software training tool for IBM.
- Led Lotus' entry into the small business market segment through managing product development and the launch of the 1-2-3 Small Business Kit and the Lotus spreadsheet for DeskMate.

I look forward to hearing from you.

Sincerely,

Chris Smith

Chris Smith

RESPONSE TO A CLASSIFIED ADVERTISEMENT
Newspaper Intern

178 Green Street
Charlotsville, VA 22906
csmith@netmail.com

April 7, 2001

Pat Cummings
Managing Editor
Any Newspaper
1140 Main Street
Lexington, VA 24450

Dear Mr. Cummings:

I enclose my resume in response to your listing in the University of Virginia's career services office for a internship position with your newspaper. I am currently a junior majoring in English at UVA, and am seeking valuable career experience for the months of June through mid-September. I am hoping to use this summer to explore possible opportunities within the field of newspaper publishing.

The position you outline is one I feel I could enhance with my writing, editing, and expressive skills gained as an English major, as well as my past work experience, which has involved a great deal of organization, discipline, and responsibility. My active leadership and service roles have also helped me develop strong interpersonal and communication skills which I feel would make me a worthy addition to your staff.

I would greatly appreciate the opportunity to discuss with you how I might best meet your needs. I will call your office next week to confirm receipt of my resume and inquire about the publicized opening. In the interim, if you have any questions, please do not hesitate to call me at (804) 555-5555.

Thank you for your consideration in this matter.

Sincerely yours,

Chris Smith

Chris Smith

RESPONSE TO A CLASSIFIED ADVERTISEMENT
Occupational Health Manager

178 Green Street
Des Plaines, IL 60016
(708) 555-5555

July 26, 2001

Pat Cummings
Vice-President, Managerial
Any Corporation
1140 Main Street
Indianapolis, IN 46206

Dear Ms. Cummings:

My interest in the position of Occupational Health Manager recently advertised in the *Indianapolis Star* has prompted me to forward my resume for your consideration.

In addition to my experience as a certified occupational health nurse and hands-on clinical expertise, I have twenty-one years of experience in positions which involved autonomous responsibility for the development and implementation of occupational health programs. All of these positions required sound knowledge of OSHA and general occupational health issues in critical work areas.

I received several commendations for my dedication and professionalism, and continually received recognition for my communication skills and leadership excellence. Based on my qualifications, I believe I am the right person to oversee the delivery of occupational health services for one or more of your clients.

Thank you for your consideration.

Sincerely,

Chris Smith

Chris Smith, R.N.

RESPONSE TO A CLASSIFIED ADVERTISEMENT
Office Receptionist

178 Green Street
Gastonia, NC 28054
(704) 555-5555

January 16, 2001

Pat Cummings
Personnel Supervisor
Any Corporation
1140 Main Street
Mt. Olive, NC 28465

Dear Mr. Cummings:

I am interested in applying for the receptionist position advertised in the *Herald Sun*.

I enjoy customer/client interaction and believe that an organization's client relationships are a tangible asset in a world where individualized service and assistance is rapidly declining. My administrative skills include a 70 wpm typing speed and proficiency on multiple word processing programs and spreadsheet applications.

I look forward to hearing from you.

Sincerely,

Chris Smith

Chris Smith

RESPONSE TO A CLASSIFIED ADVERTISEMENT
Park Maintenance Supervisor

178 Green Street
Zanesville, OH 43701
(614) 555-5555

August 28, 2001

Pat Cummings
Chairperson
Any Reservation
1140 Main Street
Youngstown, OH 44501

Dear Ms. Cummings:

Please accept the enclosed resume as my expressed interest in applying for the park maintenance position advertised in the *Vindicator*. For the past twelve years, I have held a senior-level position as fire chief of the Zanesville Fire Department.

Although my position is secure, it is strictly administrative and does not allow me to physically participate, as I have in the past, in actual firefighting or other hands-on activities that provide the outdoor work environment I most enjoy. For some time I have realized that I must make a change, and the position described in your advertisement is what I have been looking for.

I have worked on a family farm, attended a degree program in agriculture, and by choice have always worked full-time or part-time with tree and excavation services. I am thoroughly familiar with the operation, maintenance, and repair of equipment, including safety practices. I also have the necessary background to train and supervise work crews using this equipment. I feel confident that I can provide Any Reservation with reliability, dedication, and quality performance.

Since the department is not aware of my interest in making a change, your confidence is appreciated. I look forward to your response.

Yours,

Chris Smith

Chris Smith

RESPONSE TO A CLASSIFIED ADVERTISEMENT
Photographer/Writer

178 Green Street
Poughkeepsie, NY 12601
(601) 555-5555
csmith@netmail.com

July 22, 2001

Pat Cummings
Human Resources Director
Any Corporation
1140 Main Street
Bellingham, WA 98225

Dear Mr. Cummings:

I am responding to the advertisement in the *Seattle Times* for a photographer/writer.

I am an accomplished photographer with over ten years' experience in commercial and industrial photography, portraiture, and wedding photography. I hold a Bachelor of Arts in English from Clark College, where relevant coursework included feature writing, photojournalism, and news reporting.

I have attended seminars and workshops with the Fred Jones Workshop and the Winona School of Professional Photography. My photos have appeared in the Winona course catalog, BBI Printing Company's catalog, and numerous Smithco publications (including annual reports and newsletters).

My published writings include *A Shutterbug's Notes* and *Picture Your Pet.*

I look forward to hearing from you if my qualifications meet your needs.

Thank you.

Sincerely,

Chris Smith

Chris Smith

RESPONSE TO A CLASSIFIED ADVERTISEMENT
Political Staffer

178 Green Street
Bristol, RI 02809
(401) 555-5555

January 25, 2001

Pat Cummings
Director
Any Organization
1140 Main Street
Providence, RI 02908

Dear Ms. Cummings:

   I am responding to the Political Staffer position advertised in the January 24 edition of the *Providence Evening Bulletin*.

   Currently, I am employed as an Administrative Assistant at the State House in Providence. My primary responsibilities include writing press releases, researching and drafting legislation, and consistent constituent contact. I have also worked with various committees and legislators regarding an array of legislative issues.

   I hold a Bachelor of Arts from Boston University in Political Science with a concentration in Public Policy. In addition to my coursework at BU, I worked as an intern at the Lieutenant Governor's office during the spring of 1999 and actively worked for several political and social causes on campus and in the Boston area. I also organized and managed my own successful campaign for Secretary of Student Affairs.

   I am eager to continue my political career in the position of Staffer for your organization. I have the commitment, energy, and drive necessary to contribute successfully to your cause.

   Thank you for your consideration.

Sincerely,

Chris Smith

Chris Smith

RESPONSE TO A CLASSIFIED ADVERTISEMENT
Preschool Director

178 Green Street
St. Paul, MN 55105
(612) 555-5555

July 10, 2001

Pat Cummings
Principal
Any High School
1140 Main Street
Minneapolis, MN 55404

Dear Mr. Cummings:

As a speech and language clinician with extensive experience in managing and administering programs dealing with special needs in education, I feel I have the qualifications for the preschool director position advertised in the *Star Tribune*.

During the past eleven years, my experience with a professional, private agency has been concentrated in the area of special needs programs for multiple school districts. Prior to that, my work as a speech and language clinician involved developing and implementing special-education programs for preschoolers through twelfth grade in a public school system.

I look forward to hearing from you if my qualifications meet your needs.

Yours sincerely,

Chris Smith

Chris Smith

RESPONSE TO A CLASSIFIED ADVERTISEMENT
Product Developer

178 Green Street
Bismarck, ND 58501
(701) 555-5555
csmith@netmail.com

February 15, 2001

Pat Cummings
Chief Executive Officer
Any Technology
1140 Main Street
Bismarck, ND 58501

Dear Ms. Cummings:

I read with much excitement in your company newsletter the announcement of openings within your new products development department.

Please note that I have more than ten years of experience in manufacturing R&D, management of new product development, and existing product redevelopment/upgrade. I am especially experienced with complex composite materials, precision metal castings, and PC board industries. In addition, I have extensive experience both as teacher and lecturer at several well-known universities. This expertise is supported by a Ph.D. in Materials Science/Engineering.

I am eager to join the Any Technology team. Thank you for your consideration.

Sincerely,

Chris Smith

Chris Smith

RESPONSE TO A CLASSIFIED ADVERTISEMENT
Production Assistant

178 Green Street
Birmingham, AL 35294
(205) 555-5555

October 2, 2001

Pat Cummings
Vice-President, Production
Any Corporation
1146 Main Street
Mobile, AL 36630

RE: Production Assistant Position

Dear Mr. Cummings:

Your recent advertisement in the *Mobile Register* interests me, as my experience matches your requirements.

I would appreciate the opportunity to discuss how I might contribute to your organization. I will call your office the week of October 10th to schedule an interview at your convenience. In the meantime, I may be reached at the above listed daytime phone number or in the evenings at (205) 555-5555.

Thank you for your consideration.

Sincerely,

Chris Smith

Chris Smith

RESPONSE TO A CLASSIFIED ADVERTISEMENT
Production Controller

178 Green Street
Pittsburgh, PA 15217
(412) 555-5555

February 23, 2001

Pat Cummings
Hiring Manager
Any Corporation
1140 Main Street
Boston, MA 02215

RE: Production Controller

Dear Ms. Cummings:

After seven years of progressively responsible experience in production, electro-mechanical assembly, soldering, testing, total quality management, and shipping and receiving a precision manufacturing operation, I feel I have all the qualifications you require for the above advertised position.

During the past several years, my responsibilities as Group Leader necessitated that I provide a harmonious work atmosphere. While accomplishing this objective, I developed training procedures which allowed for cross-training, multiethnic, multicultural, production personnel to work at ten assembly stations. This assured that all stations could be covered despite employee absences. In addition, I implemented TQM, which resulted in a 40 percent increase in productivity, a 20 percent decrease in production costs, and a flurry of letters from satisfied clients.

I am aware of Any Corporation's innovative approach to TQM, which has been used as an example across the country. I desire the opportunity to apply manufacturing know-how to the smooth running of your production operations.

Thank you for reviewing my credentials.

Yours sincerely,

Chris Smith

Chris Smith

RESPONSE TO A CLASSIFIED ADVERTISEMENT
Program Coordinator

178 Green Street
Holland, MI 49423
(616) 555-5555

September 30, 2001

Pat Cummings
Language Coordinator
Any Institute
1140 Main Street
Detroit, MI 48226

Dear Mr. Cummings:

I would like to apply for the ESL program coordinator position advertised in the *Detroit Free Press*. I am particularly qualified for this job as a result of my double language major in college and my current enrollment in two language proficiency certificate programs.

Having grown up in a bilingual (Spanish/English-speaking) environment and having studied abroad in both Spain and Mexico, I am aware of the demands and technical challenges involved in translations. To meet these challenges and maintain my skills, I work on my languages weekly, both by continuing to take language classes and by tutoring children in the fundamentals.

I hope to have the opportunity to discuss my qualifications with you further.

Sincerely,

Chris Smith

Chris Smith

RESPONSE TO A CLASSIFIED ADVERTISEMENT
Project Manager

178 Green Street
Charleston, SC 29411
(803) 555-5555

April 10, 2001

Pat Cummings
Director of Human Resources
Any Corporation
1140 Main Street
Charleston, SC 29411

Dear Ms. Cummings:

In response to your ad for Project Manager in the April 9 edition of the *Post and Courier*, I have enclosed my resume for your review and consideration.

With over twenty years of construction experience, I am familiar with project management in the role of owner's representative as well as general contractor/manager. I have managed projects regionally and nationally.

I look forward to discussing my credentials and the requirements of the position with you.

Sincerely,

Chris Smith

Chris Smith

RESPONSE TO A CLASSIFIED ADVERTISEMENT
Public Relations Associate

178 Green Street
Keuka Park, NY 14478
(315) 555-5555

May 2, 2001

Pat Cummings
Vice-President
Any Firm
1140 Main Street
Riverdale, NJ 10471

Dear Mr. Cummings:

In response to your advertisement in the *New York Times* for the Public Relations Associate position, I would like to touch on particular aspects of my background that should be of interest to you.

Between 1994 and 1998, I supervised (as a civilian employee) the internal formation and public relations programs for the U.S. Army in Frankfurt, Germany. As Director of Information Services, I was responsible for writing and publishing internal publications, brochures, and other communications. I also edited a community newspaper and magazine during this time.

For two years prior to that association, I edited a variety of military publications, both newspapers and magazines, while serving as a member of the uniformed services in Germany. During this period, I wrote news, sports, and feature articles as well as press releases. I conducted media events, prepared slide presentations, gave briefings, and designed other internal and external promotional materials in support of the 7th Infantry Division and its 30,000 American soldiers and family members in four German communities.

In 1998, I returned to the United States and completed work for my Master of Arts in Communications from Rutgers University. Prior to my relocation, I managed an annual budget of $500,000 while supervising a staff of eight in the Connecticut gaming industry. I also wrote promotional articles for the casino in the local newspaper.

I look forward to discussing my background and experience in detail with you and would be glad to make myself available for an interview at your convenience.

Sincerely yours,

Chris Smith

Chris Smith

RESPONSE TO A CLASSIFIED ADVERTISEMENT
Publicist

178 Green Street
East Point, GA 30344
(404) 555-5555

February 4, 2001

Pat Cummings
Publicity Director
Any Corporation
1140 Main Street
Rome, GA 30162

Dear Ms. Cummings:

I am responding to your advertisement in the *Atlanta Constitution* for a Publicist.

I am confident that I have the skills and experience necessary to successfully meet the requirements of this position. As an Advertising and Promotions Assistant for a major newspaper, I have acquired strong interpersonal and communication skills. In addition, I have extensive experience with a number of computer systems and applications.

As the newest member of your publicity department, I would prove to be a diligent, organized, and enthusiastic employee. Could we meet for further discussion? I would be available at your convenience.

I look forward to your response.

Sincerely,

Chris Smith

Chris Smith

RESPONSE TO A CLASSIFIED ADVERTISEMENT
Publisher's Assistant

178 Green Street
Topeka, KS 66621
(913) 555-5555

January 18, 2001

Pat Cummings
Vice-President of Editorial
Any Corporation
1140 Main Street
Topeka, KS 66621

Dear Mr. Cummings:

I am writing in response to your advertisement in the *Topeka Capital-Journal* for the Publisher's Assistant position. Please consider me an applicant for the position.

I believe you will find that my training and varied experience are well suited for this position. My background as an administrative assistant, magazine production assistant, and teacher demonstrate my capacity to handle the challenges of providing superior executive support.

As a current temporary assignment worker with Alltemps in Topeka, I have become highly computer literate in both Macintosh and IBM environments and accompanying software programs. I am organized and accurate, master new information rapidly, communicate effectively, and work well with other people.

Thank you for reviewing my credentials. I will call in a week to schedule a convenient time to discuss my qualifications and your expectations.

Sincerely,

Chris Smith

Chris Smith

RESPONSE TO A CLASSIFIED ADVERTISEMENT
Purchasing Agent

178 Green Street
Grove Village, IL 60007
(708) 555-5555

February 4, 2001

Employment Manager
Any Corporation
1140 Main Street
Chicago, IL 60628

Dear Ms. Cummings:

Please accept this letter and resume as an application for the purchasing agent position advertised in the *Macon Telegraph*.

I have six years' experience, ranging from purchasing clerk to senior buyer for multisite operations, with purchases in excess of $1.5 million. I have been a key contributor to the successful setup and startup of new branch locations, from bare walls to fully trained and operating facility.

I appreciate your consideration of my application and look forward to your reply.

Sincerely,

Chris Smith

Chris Smith

RESPONSE TO A CLASSIFIED ADVERTISEMENT
Real Estate Sales Associate

178 Green Street
Milwaukee, WI 53201
(414) 555-5555

December 20, 2001

Pat Cummings
Vice-President
Any Properties
1140 Main Street
Milwaukee, WI 53201

RE: Advertisement in Real Estate Weekly, December 20, 2001

Dear Mr. Cummings:

I am writing to apply for the above-listed position. I am interested in contributing my real estate expertise to Any Properties.

I offer nearly twenty years of intensive experience involving the most sophisticated aspects of commercial and residential real estate sales and leasing, as well as associated areas of real estate development, property management, and rehabilitation. In addition to a current brokers' license, I am very well grounded in real estate and business law.

I am considered a highly organized team player, with excellent verbal and written communications skills, an eye for detail, and the necessary persistence to conceive, package, and bring the big deals home.

Thank you for your consideration.

Sincerely,

Chris Smith

Chris Smith

RESPONSE TO A CLASSIFIED ADVERTISEMENT
Regional Manager

178 Green Street
Dubuque, IA 52001
(319) 555-5555
csmith@netmail.com

August 7, 2001

Pat Cummings
Management Supervisor
Any Corporation
1140 Main Street
Peosta, IA 52068

Dear Ms. Cummings:

Please accept this inquiry as my expressed interest in the Regional Manager position advertised in the August issue of *Automotive Monthly*.

During the past twenty-two years, I have developed a successful track record as a professional with internationally recognized expertise in the automotive industries. In the last twelve years, I have specialized in customer satisfaction program development and strategic implementation consulting.

My extensive management experience has encompassed the design and evaluation of corporate marketing strategies and involved the evaluation of policies, projects, and new products. This experience is supported by a B.A. in Economics, an M.A. in Economics, M.B.A. coursework, a D.Sc., and a D.E.S. in Applied Mathematics.

Although my present position provides interesting diversity and challenge, I feel that it is time to move on to other opportunities.

Thank you for your consideration.

Sincerely,

Chris Smith

Chris Smith

RESPONSE TO A CLASSIFIED ADVERTISEMENT
Researcher

178 Green Street
Washington, DC 20057
(202) 555-5555
csmith@netmail.com

October 31, 2001

Pat Cummings
Human Resources Director
Any Newspaper
1140 Main Street
Chicago, IL 60605

Dear Mr. Cummings:

I am writing in response to the researcher position advertised in the *Washington Post*.

I have been a reporter for magazines and newspapers for many years and have authored or coauthored five books on sports and communications. I have written over 3,500 articles for publication, on topics ranging from crime and sports to medicine and humor. I know how to conceive of and research topics, and I am comfortable writing on almost any subject and in a range of styles. I am confident I would have no trouble matching the established style of your book series.

I have copyedited a number of books on business topics and have worked as an editor for several newspapers. I am capable of doing either minor polishing or major rewriting and, more important, of being able to tell which job is needed. In addition, I taught English Composition and Writing for the Print Media at the high school level for five years.

Enclosed are a resume and a brief writing sample.

I look forward to hearing from you.

Sincerely,

Chris Smith

Chris Smith

RESPONSE TO A CLASSIFIED ADVERTISEMENT
Restaurant Manager Trainee

178 Green Street
Grand Junction, CO 81502
(303) 555-5555

November 15, 2001

Pat Cummings
Manager
Any Restaurant
1140 Main Street
Denver Post, CO 80202

Dear Ms. Cummings:

Please accept the enclosed resume as application for the restaurant manager trainee position advertised in the *Denver Post*.

During the past seven years, I have held positions of responsibility in banquet and special event catering, function management, and restaurant food service operations. I have additional experience in front-desk operation. I have good organizational, leadership, training, and supervisory skills and can provide quality service and performance in a high-volume setting.

I have continually heard and read many favorable reviews of Any Restaurant, and I have always enjoyed my own dining experiences there. I would be interested in joining your management team after completing the requisite training program and hope you will give me the opportunity to discuss this further.

Sincerely,

Chris Smith

Chris Smith

RESPONSE TO A CLASSIFIED ADVERTISEMENT
Sales Representative

178 Green Street
Northridge, CA 91324
(818) 555-5555

April 17, 2001

Ms. Pat Cummings
Vice-President
Any Corporation
1140 Main Street
Pittsburgh, PA 15217

Dear Mr. Cummings:

I would like to apply for the position of sales representative advertised in the *Pittsburgh Post-Gazette*.

I have several years' experience in developing sales and marketing strategies. I have been involved in a number of employment situations, including a self-owned business, in which I successfully applied sales techniques, including cold calling, telemarketing, and prospecting. In my first two years at FloSoft, I increased the client base by 25 percent. While at the Brian Agency, I was part of a sales team that generated a record-breaking $10 million in one year. In addition, I have held numerous positions where I supervised and developed personnel and assisted in facilitating daily operations.

I hope you will give me the opportunity to speak with you about the available position. Thank you for your time and consideration.

With best regards,

Chris Smith

Chris Smith

RESPONSE TO A CLASSIFIED ADVERTISEMENT
Senior HVAC Technician

178 Green Street
New Martinsville, WV 26155
(304) 555-5555

November 12, 2001

Pat Cummings
Human Resources Director
Any Corporation
1140 Main Street
Charlestown, WV 25301

Dear Ms. Cummings:

At the request of Donald Lee of your department, I am enclosing my resume in answer to the advertisement in last Friday's *Charleston Gazette* for an experienced Senior HVAC Technician.

I possess nine years of experience in after-warranty maintenance, preventive maintenance programs, and complete overhaul of major systems within a multibuilding, mixed-use industrial complex. I have also completed extensive and continuous education and training on the latest and most cost-efficient energy systems and control.

Presently, I am seeking a new association with an institution such as Any Corporation where I can apply my technical as well as supervisory skills to provide quality, cost-efficient, energy control system maintenance at a time when energy prices are at an all-time high.

I would welcome the opportunity to discuss your requirements and my ability to handle the responsibilities of the position offered. Could we meet for a personal interview? I can make myself readily available whenever you are free.

Sincerely,

Chris Smith

Chris Smith

RESPONSE TO A CLASSIFIED ADVERTISEMENT
Site Location Supervisor

178 Green Street
Smithfield, RI 02917

April 16, 2001

Pat Cummings
General Manager, Properties
Any Corporation
1140 Main Street
Bridgeville, PA 15017

RE: Executive Position, Site Location and Store Build-Outs

Dear Mr. Cummings:

I am confident that I am the person you seek in your advertisement in the April 15 edition of the *Providence Evening Bulletin*. My interest is in joining a firm which has a need for a representative capable of working effectively with clients in real estate development, property management, and finance. Because of a broad and diverse background, I am well qualified to provide consulting and/or management services to clients with problems involving planning, financing, budgeting, scheduling, and monitoring any phase of development-related activity.

During the past fifteen years, my experience as a developer, general manager, owner, and manager of residential, commercial, and industrial projects has been extensive. In conjunction with these projects, I was actively involved in investment analysis, whole loans and structured transactions, and financial control to assure quality completion within schedules and budgets.

I relate well to individuals and groups at all levels of responsibility and can fulfill management responsibilities while expediting project completions from inception to final inspection.

Although my resume is enclosed, I would be able to provide you with additional pertinent information as to my capabilities and goals during a personal interview. I am free to relocate and/or travel and the compensation package is negotiable. I can be reached at the above address or by phone at (401) 555-5555.

Sincerely,

Chris Smith

Chris Smith

RESPONSE TO A CLASSIFIED ADVERTISEMENT
Social Worker

178 Green Street
Northridge, CA 91324
(818) 555-5555

July 19, 2001

Pat Cummings
Director
Any Agency
1140 Main Street
Northridge, CA 91324

Dear Ms. Cummings:

In response to your advertisement in the summer edition of the *Social Justice Journal*, I would like to offer my services to fill the vacancy in the Social Worker position. I am confident you will find my experience and abilities qualify me for the position.

I possess extensive diverse and applicable experience. As stated in my resume, I received a bachelor's degree in Dance Therapy, an interdisciplinary major, which involved extensive research into child psychology as well as artistic ability. While in college, I worked with children in a volunteer program called P.A.L.S, in which we visited and recreated with children in housing projects. I also visited a day-care program to study the psychology behind children's drawings for my senior research project. In addition, in high school, I worked with mentally disturbed adults.

As you can see, my background corresponds to your requirements. I look forward to hearing from you to discuss this job further.

Sincerely,

Chris Smith

Chris Smith

RESPONSE TO A CLASSIFIED ADVERTISEMENT
State Administrator

178 Green Street
Riverside, CA 92521
(909) 555-5555

December 23, 2001

Pat Cummings
President, New England Offices
Any Organization
1140 Main Street
Sacramento, CA 95821

Dear Mr. Cummings:

In response to your advertisement in the December 20 edition of the *Sacramento Bee*, please find my resume enclosed for your review. I am very interested in securing the position of State Administrator available at Any Organization.

During the past twelve years, I have held diverse and progressively responsible positions in development for nonprofit service organizations, universities, and educational institutions. These responsibilities have ranged from Secretary to Director of Development.

Throughout this period, I have been heavily involved in development strategies, annual fund campaigns, marketing and mailing programs, and media and public relations. Although these positions have been challenging and broad in scope, I feel that my expertise may be utilized to a better advantage by your organization.

I hope that, after reviewing my qualifications, you will consider me as the right candidate for State Administrator. I am confident of my abilities, and would like to schedule an interview to reiterate my desire for the position.

I appreciate your time and look forward to speaking with you.

Sincerely,

Chris Smith

Chris Smith

RESPONSE TO A CLASSIFIED ADVERTISEMENT
Store Manager

178 Green Street
New Haven, CT 06520
(203) 555-5555

December 22, 2001

Pat Cummings
District Supervisor
Any Corporation
1140 Main Street
Jacksonville, FL 32231

Dear Ms. Cummings:

In response to your advertisement for a Store Manager in the December 15 edition of the *Sarasota Herald-Tribune*, I am forwarding my resume. As detailed below, my experience qualifies me for the position.

You require:
- Managerial experience
- Superior written and verbal skills
- Budget management abilities

I offer:
- Five years as senior manager in a chain bookstore with an annual volume in excess of $2 million. Ability to manage inventory, personnel, cash flow.
- Accreditation as a high school teacher. Recognition for "Where We're At," a light-hearted historical essay.
- At University Towers, decreased outstanding rents by $5,000. Reorganized Sturtevant's retail promotions, effecting a 50 percent budget reduction.

May we discuss how I may contribute to your organization? I am available at your convenience to discuss employment opportunities, and the possibility of relocation.

Thank you for reviewing my credentials. I look forward to hearing from you.

Sincerely,

Chris Smith

Chris Smith

RESPONSE TO A CLASSIFIED ADVERTISEMENT
Systems Trainer

178 Green Street
Natchitoches, LA 71497
(318) 555-5555

July 16, 2001

Pat Cummings
Director
Any Corporation
1140 Main Street
Lafayette, LA 70504

Dear Mr. Cummings:

In response to your advertisement in the *Times*, I would like to apply for the position of systems trainer.

I have extensive experience in managing in-house and client training services on state-of-the-art systems, using technical and business applications. In addition to a Bachelor of Science in Education and postgraduate study in computer science and business, I have nine years of project and senior management experience with concentration in training, documentation, and related companywide services for business and technical environments. I have hands-on experience with many software and hardware systems and can implement cost-effective, efficient breakthroughs in systems and training.

I look forward to hearing from you.

Sincerely,

Chris Smith

Chris Smith

RESPONSE TO A CLASSIFIED ADVERTISEMENT
Technical Writer

178 Green Street
Santa Fe, NM 87501
(505) 555-5555
csmith@netmail.com

July 22, 2001

Pat Cummings
Publicity Director
Any Tech
1140 Main Street
Santa Fe, NM 87501

Dear Ms. Cummings:

I would like to apply for the technical writer position advertised in *Engineering World*.

I am currently employed as a technical writer at Computer Systems International. We release three documentation sets for software: user guides, references, and batch operations and sample reports.

My past work includes newspaper and freelance writing. Since graduating from the University of Maine with a Journalism/English degree, I have edited manuscripts for medical and scientific publications. At the *Albuquerque Journal*, as a sports editor and general assignment writer/photographer, I wrote sports and news articles and features. I also took and processed photographs and designed pages. As a staff writer at MediaCorps, I prepared press packages on new products.

I hope to be able to discuss the available position with you further.

Sincerely,

Chris Smith

Chris Smith

RESPONSE TO A CLASSIFIED ADVERTISEMENT
Telemarketer

178 Green Street
Omaha, NE 68182
(402) 555-5555

January 22, 2001

Pat Cummings
Director of Marketing and Sales
Any Corporation
1140 Main Street
Lincoln, NE 68522
Dear Mr. Cummings:

I am responding to your advertisement in search of a telemarketing professional in the *Lincoln Journal* dated January 16.

The enclosed resume provides details of my solid career experience in marketing and sales. My accomplishments include:

- Managing and directing sales of a national publication to business decision-makers and chief executive officers of major financial, educational and municipal leaders which resulted in $175,000 sales in a four-month period.
- Creating and implementing marketing strategy of a family-owned retail establishment which produced substantial increase in sales.
- Establishing a marketing and public relations plan for a consulting firm which increased client base and significantly enhanced public recognition of firm.
- Writing, editing, directing, and producing public service television program which involved timely legal and medical issues.

I would be pleased to discuss this matter with you in a personal interview and look forward to hearing from you.

Sincerely,

Chris Smith

Chris Smith

RESPONSE TO A CLASSIFIED ADVERTISEMENT
Television Camera Operator

178 Green Street
Pineville, LA 71359
(318) 555-5555

January 18, 2001

Pat Cummings
Production Manager
Any Television Station
1140 Main Street
New Orleans, LA 70018

Dear Ms. Cummings:

When I read your job description for a Television Camera Operator in the *Sunday Times-Picayune*, I felt that my background and skills would be a wonderful match for your requirements.

During the past three years, I have worked extensively as a Production Assistant and Technical Operator in a television studio involving all aspects of video production. I also have written, directed, produced, and edited three short 8 mm films and a music video which was shot using ENG equipment. These projects allowed me to sharpen many skills, such as conceptualization, camera work, and editing. In addition, I have received a Bachelor of Science and gained additional experience in video and camera operation from Ellis Technical Training School.

Once given the opportunity to demonstrate my talents, I am sure that I can prove to be a worthwhile addition to your station. Also, I am confident of my ability to quickly excel through a training program and soon begin taping. I look forward to the opportunity for an interview and to meet with you in person.

Sincerely,

Chris Smith

Chris Smith

RESPONSE TO A CLASSIFIED ADVERTISEMENT
Translator

178 Green Street
Lawrenceville, GA 30246
(404) 555-5555

June 2, 2001

Pat Cummings
Head Translator
Any Organization
1140 Main Street
Atlanta, GA 30318

Dear Mr. Cummings:

I am writing in response to your May 30th advertisement in the *Atlanta Constitution* for a Translator. I was immediately intrigued by this position and would like to be considered in your search.

I am convinced that my interest, combined with my experience, could be well utilized by your organization. While completing my Bachelor of Science at Emory University, I worked as a Translating Assistant in the translation center on campus. My duties included translating documents from both Spanish and Russian into English and vice versa, verbally communicating with international contacts, and entering and editing articles and poetry for publication. It should be noted that several of the articles were in foreign languages I do not speak, which required very strong attention to detail in their translation.

While at Emory, I spent a semester studying abroad in St. Petersburg, Russia. As a personal tutor, I developed lessons for English instruction to foreign students. This unique opportunity, as well as my extensive travel throughout Latin America, allowed me to sharpen my verbal and written Russian and Spanish translation skills.

I believe my experience and knowledge would successfully be applied to the Translator position you are seeking to fill. Thank you for your time and I look forward to meeting with you.

Sincerely,

Chris Smith

Chris Smith

RESPONSE TO A CLASSIFIED ADVERTISEMENT
Travel Agent

178 Green Street
New Britain, CT 06050
(203) 555-5555

January 29, 2001

Pat Cummings
Owner
Any Travel Agency
1140 Main Street
New London, CT 06320

Dear Ms. Cummings:

I would like to apply for the position of travel agent advertised in the *Wichita Eagle*.

As my resume indicates, I have eleven years' experience in the travel and tourism fields. As sole owner of a tourism-related business for four years, I oversaw and advised thirty host homes and inns operating in New England. I was independently responsible for maintaining accurate business records, purchasing supplies, and writing and editing all public relations materials, contracts, and policy guidelines.

In addition, my associations with the Greater Connecticut Convention and Visitor's Bureau, the Southern Connecticut Bureau, and the Connecticut Chamber of Commerce have heightened my awareness of visitor markets and related disposable income.

I look forward to hearing from you if my qualifications meet your needs. Thank you for your consideration.

Sincerely,

Chris Smith

Chris Smith

RESPONSE TO A CLASSIFIED ADVERTISEMENT
Writing Instructor

178 Green Street
Richmond, VA 23219
(804) 555-5555

June 1, 2001

Pat Cummings
Dean
Any College
1140 Main Street
Winston-Salem, NC 27108

Dear Mr. Cummings:

Please consider this letter and the enclosed resume as an application for the position of Writing Instructor as advertised in the *Richmond Times-Dispatch* last Wednesday.

I have been a college-level teacher of writing for the past eleven years and offer strong writing, editing, and proofreading skills. I am also a writer; my published works include short stories, essays, and poems. Last February, a one-act play of mine was produced in New York City. I also have experience ghostwriting, editing for the Chapel Hill Review, and publicity writing for a Raleigh rock group.

I am confident that the above-listed experience distinguishes me as a qualified candidate for your opening. I would be delighted to discuss further how my abilities match your requirements.

Thanks for your attention to this matter.

Sincerely,

Chris Smith

Chris Smith

RESPONSE TO A CLASSIFIED ADVERTISEMENT
Yacht Salesperson

178 Green Street
San Francisco, CA 94132
(415) 555-5555

June 6, 2001

Pat Cummings
Vice-President, Sales
Any Corporation
1140 Main Street
Modesto, CA 95354

Dear Ms. Cummings:

If you are looking for an energetic, dedicated representative for the position in yacht sales you advertised in the *Modesto Bee*, I believe we have good reason to meet.

In addition to a Bachelor of Arts in Business Administration and Marketing, I have several years of successful experience in advertising, promoting, and selling high-priced properties to clients in the upper income bracket. My experience and extensive travel as a co-host at international and domestic conferences, attended by government and business leaders, required refined communication skills and the ability to effectively negotiate with high-level decision-makers.

I would like to utilize these skills within Any Corporation to penetrate markets and increase sales of big-ticket items such as yachts. I am willing to travel, and believe that I will, through my persistent efforts, meet, and even exceed, mutual sales objectives.

Enclosed please find my resume. I am very interested in learning more about the position and how my qualifications might suit you.

Sincerely,

Chris Smith

Chris Smith

RESPONSE TO A CLASSIFIED ADVERTISEMENT
Youth Center Director

178 Green Street
Tuscaloosa, AL 35401
(205) 555-5555

August 20, 2001

Pat Cummings
Regional Director
Any Youth Center
1140 Main Street
Palo Alto, CA 94203

Dear Mr. Cummings:

I would like to apply for the executive director position advertised in the *Los Angeles Times*.

During the past two years, I have researched and developed a new youth center in Tuscaloosa County. Thus far, I have developed programs serving over fifteen hundred individuals and families, with a budget size almost doubling in one year. My experience also includes grant and proposal writing, public relations, board and committee development, and community and corporate presentations.

I hope you will give me the opportunity to speak to you about the available position.
I appreciate your consideration.

Sincerely,

Chris Smith

Chris Smith

RESPONSE TO A "BLIND" ADVERTISEMENT
Applications Programmer

178 Green Street
Harrisburg, PA 17101
(717) 555-5555
csmith@netmail.com

February 20, 2001

P.O. Box 7777
Harrisburg, PA 17101

Dear Sir or Madam:

If you have a need for a competent programmer analyst with expertise in application development, maintenance, and enhancement of programs in purchasing, inventory control, contracts management, and related logistics applications, then please consider my credentials.

During the past thirteen years, I have handled projects for Agtech and CompWare that require the ability to work effectively with large systems as well as PC-based software environments. I have extensive experience developing, maintaining, and enhancing programs, particularly procurement and logistics. Most of these have required interaction with various departments and users.

I hope to have the opportunity to speak to you further about the available position.

I look forward to hearing from you.

Yours,

Chris Smith

Chris Smith

RESPONSE TO A "BLIND" ADVERTISEMENT
Assistant Personnel Officer

178 Green Street
Vienna, VA 22211
(703) 555-5555

June 1, 2001

Human Resources Director
P.O. Box 7777
Arlington, VA 22203

Dear Sir or Madam:

I am writing to express my interest in the assistant personnel officer position advertised in the *Washington Post*.

As my resume indicates, I have extensive experience in personnel, including my most recent position as assistant staff manager at Virginia General Hospital. In this capacity I recruited and trained administrative and clerical staffs, ancillary and works department staffs, and professional and technical staffs. I also evaluated personnel, conducted disciplinary and grievance interviews, signed employees to contracts, and advised staff on conditions of employment, entitlements, and maternity leave.

I look forward to hearing from you if my qualifications meet your needs.

Sincerely,

Chris Smith

Chris Smith

RESPONSE TO A "BLIND" ADVERTISEMENT
Business Consultant

178 Green Street
Dedham, MA 02026
(617) 555-5555
csmith@netmail.com

March 29, 2001

Human Resources Director
P.O. Box 7777
Cincinnati, OH 45221

Dear Sir or Madam:

I am responding to your advertisement for a business consultant in the *Wall Street Journal*. It is likely that my consulting and executive experience with small businesses matches the requirements for the position.

In 1994, while general manager of Kimcorp, I developed an extension to the company's core production services business: a fast-turnaround, low-cost (and high-margin) circuit proto-typing service. In addition, I conceived of the functional specifications of a software package that would help designers do board layout on their PCs. Since then I have remained involved with computers in business and consulting activities.

I hope to have the opportunity to speak with you further about this position.

Sincerely,

Chris Smith

Chris Smith

178 Green Street
Alfred, NY 14802
(607) 555-5555

October 28, 2001

P.O. Box 7777
Conway, SC 29526

Dear Sir or Madam:

I would like to apply for the legal associate position advertised in *Lawyers Weekly*. As you will note from my resume, I hold a Juris Doctor degree and recently received a Master of Law in Banks and Banking Law Studies, with a concentration in International Law.

Aside from familiarity with all phases of research, document preparation, and coordination, I have experience supervising associate and support legal staff. One case I worked on for the defense was *Acme v. Smith*. After the surprise decision for the defense, Jack Robinson, the defense co-counsel, sent me a letter in which he said, "I want to thank you for your significant contribution to a well-prepared case."

I also have experience with maritime issues and international law pertaining to shipping. I have dealt with several foreign shipping lines regarding bulk transport of oil, grain, and other commodities, as well as customs procedures and matters involving the Coast Guard.

If my qualifications meet your needs, I hope you will give me the opportunity to speak to you further about the available position.

Sincerely,

Chris Smith

Chris Smith

RESPONSE TO A "BLIND" ADVERTISEMENT
Librarian

178 Green Street
Quincy, MA 02171
(781) 555-5555

July 22, 2001

Personnel Director
P.O. Box 7777
Amherst, MA 01003

Dear Sir or Madam:

I would like to apply for the position of librarian advertised in the *Sunday Globe.*

In addition to an M.L.S. degree and ALA accreditation, I have twelve years' experience as a bibliographer, acquisitions, special collections, and reference librarian, with concentration in history and additional experience in philosophy and religion. In these positions, I provide general and specialized reference services, develop and manage collections, perform faculty liaison work, and conduct bibliographic instruction sessions at the undergraduate and graduate levels. I am also experienced in assisting and training others in the use of electronic resources, including CD-ROM and networked information.

I have the ability to undertake a broad scope of responsibility and work effectively with a diverse population of students, faculty, and staff.

I hope you will give me the opportunity to speak to you further about the available position. I look forward to hearing from you.

Sincerely,

Chris Smith

Chris Smith

RESPONSE TO A "BLIND" ADVERTISEMENT
Marketing Analyst

178 Green Street
Beachwood, OH 44122
(216) 555-5555

January 2, 2001

Department of Human Resources
P.O. Box 7777
Dayton, OH 45402

Dear Sir or Madam:

I would like to apply for the marketing analyst position advertised in the *Dayton Daily News*.

I have a Bachelor of Science in Marketing and three years' experience, ranging from merchandise analyst to senior analyst with a rapid-growth, nationwide apparel retailer. I am responsible for recruiting, screening, and providing job overview and subsequent personnel training in retailing and distribution. Working with reports generated by a national computer network, I perform in-depth analyses of sales results and inventory levels, to provide the ideal merchandise mix and qualities to targeted markets. I also have experience working in private clubs, membership operations, banking, and television.

I look forward to hearing from you if my qualifications meet your needs.

Sincerely,

Chris Smith

Chris Smith

RESPONSE TO A "BLIND" ADVERTISEMENT
Payroll Supervisor

178 Green Street
Big Stone Gap, VA 24219
(703) 555-5555

June 6, 2001

Human Resources Associate
P.O. Box 7777
Richmond, VA 23219

Dear Sir or Madam:

I would like to apply for the payroll administrator position advertised in the *Richmond Times-Dispatch.*

In addition to a Bachelor of Arts in Economics, my background encompasses ten years of progressively responsible and sophisticated hands-on experience, including marketing research assistant, union benefits coordinator, human resources administrator, and payroll administrator. My present position involves coordinating payrolls from six company divisions, both weekly and biweekly.

Thank you for your consideration.

Sincerely,

Chris Smith

Chris Smith

RESPONSE TO A "BLIND" ADVERTISEMENT
Pharmaceutical Administrator

178 Green Street
Rock Springs, WY 82902
(307) 555-5555

September 6, 2001

Human Resources Representative
P.O. Box 7777
Casper, WY 82604

Dear Sir or Madam:

I would like to apply for the position of pharmaceutical administrator advertised in the *Casper Star Tribune.*

I have a master's degree in Hospital Pharmacy Administration and two related bachelor's degrees. For the past fifteen years, I have had progressively responsible experience, ranging from staff pharmacist to supervisor of a three-hundred-bed community hospital. In two of these positions, I computerized and reorganized the pharmaceutical distribution system to provide faster service with automated inventory control.

I hope to hear from you if my qualifications meet your needs.

Thank you for your time.

Sincerely,

Chris Smith

Chris Smith

CHAPTER 10

Cold Letters

"COLD" LETTER TO A POTENTIAL EMPLOYER
Administrative Assistant

178 Green Street
Delaware City, DE 19706
(302) 555-5555

January 18, 2001

Pat Cummings
Director, Human Resources
Any Corporation
1140 Main Street
New Castle, DE 19720

Dear Ms. Cummings:

I am interested in applying for an administrative assistant position with Any Corporation. I graduated in 1998 with an associate degree in Computer Information Systems from the University of Delaware.

I worked in the university's main computer room for two years and developed skills in a number of software packages on both PC and Macintosh systems. More recently, I worked as a receptionist with Cammarata Designs, where I gained exposure to all facets of administrative work: typing (60 wpm), phone contact, and customer relations.

I look forward to hearing from you if you have an administrative assistant position open at Any Corporation.

Thank you for your consideration.

Sincerely,

Chris Smith

Chris Smith

"COLD" LETTER TO A POTENTIAL EMPLOYER
Advertising Sales Associate

178 Green Street
Decatur, GA 30032
(404) 555-5555

August 26, 2001

Pat Cummings
Personnel Director
Any Corporation
1140 Main Street
Augusta, GA 30901

Dear Mr. Cummings:

Given both my sales experience and my objective of a career in the advertising industry, I would like to explore options within sales at Any Corporation.

I have been involved in sales and customer service with a major U.S. carrier for four years. I have learned the art, as well as the importance, of creating a strong rapport with clients and demonstrating outstanding customer service for successful sales. I have also learned unique approaches to problem-solving and how to deal with rejection with renewed optimism and good humor. In addition, I possess strong written, communication, and organizational skills.

I would certainly appreciate the opportunity to discuss how I can apply my skills and knowledge to benefit Any Corporation. I will call you next week to inquire about an interview.

Thank you.

Sincerely,

Chris Smith

Chris Smith

178 Green Street
Needham, MA 02192
(617) 555-5555
csmith@netmail.com

June 18, 2001

Pat Cummings
Human Resources Director
Any Publishing Company
1140 Main Street
New York, NY 10128

Dear Ms. Cummings:

I have four years of publishing experience, including two years of scholarly journal experience in social science, physical science, and engineering, that I would like to put to work at Any Publishing Company.

Specifically, I am seeking a position as an associate editor, project editor, or the equivalent in new book or journal development and administration. I am planning to relocate to the New York area later this summer. My qualifications include the following:

- Developed a new book series in sociology through all phases of publication, from author contract negation to the creation of a series marketing plan
- Acquired *Earth Day Every Day,* which was nominated for the Fortmiller Foundation's Prize and is already an academic bestseller
- Participated in a dynamic engineering program that included the launch of three new journals: *Physical Science, Micro Journal,* and the *Journal of Alternative Energy*
- In addition to a strong background in English literature and the social sciences at the University of Notre Dame, my training has included courses relevant to a position in medical publishing: anatomy, physiology, medical terminology, nursing procedures, biology, and radiographic physics.

I will be in New York from July 20-30 and wonder if I could meet with you then?

Thank you for your consideration.

Sincerely,

Chris Smith

Chris Smith

"COLD" LETTER TO A POTENTIAL EMPLOYER
Audiovisual Specialist

178 Green Street
Proctorsville, VT 05153
(802) 555-5555

July 7, 2001

Pat Cummings
Personnel Manager
Any Corporation
1140 Main Street
Chicago, IL 60605

Dear Mr. Cummings:

In the interest of investigating career opportunities with your company, I am enclosing my resume for your consideration and review.

As you will note, I have fifteen years of educational and media experience. I am proficient in operating a wide variety of photographic, video, and audio equipment. I am regularly responsible for processing, duplicating, and setting up slide presentations, including synchronized slide and audio presentations.

Thank you for your consideration. I look forward to hearing from you.

Sincerely,

Chris Smith

Chris Smith

"COLD" LETTER TO A POTENTIAL EMPLOYER
Chef

178 Green Street
Clarksville, TN 37044
(615) 555-5555

April 15, 2001

Pat Cummings
Manager
Any Hotel
1140 Main Street
Lexington, KY 40508

Dear Ms. Cummings:

I would like to inquire about culinary opportunities at Any Hotel.

During the past six years, my positions have ranged from sous chef to executive chef of a restaurant continually rated in the top one hundred restaurants and institutions nationwide. As you will note from my resume, my earlier experience includes country clubs, hotels, resorts, and four-star restaurants.

Because of my ability to organize, train, and work effectively with personnel in quality, high-volume restaurants, I am able to maintain a conscientious, highly productive work force. I have expertise in coordinating activities and directing the indoctrination and training of chefs and other kitchen staff to ensure an efficient and profitable food service.

In addition to being an honors graduate of the Culinary Institute of America, I have received several national and regional awards for my creative culinary skills.

I hope to hear from you if you have need of someone with my qualifications.

Thank you for your consideration.

Yours sincerely,

Chris Smith

Chris Smith

"COLD" LETTER TO A POTENTIAL EMPLOYER
Computer Software Designer

178 Green Street
Decorah, IA 52101
(319) 555-5555
csmith@netmail.com

February 12, 2001

Pat Cummings
Personnel Director
Any Corporation
1140 Main Street
Cedar Rapids, IA 52402

Dear Ms. Cummings:

As a graduate student completing a Master of Science in Computer Science in March of this year, I am seeking a position in application or system-oriented software.

My two years' experience as a database designer and six months' experience as an intern at Puttnee Bowles have equipped me for a position as a software designer. I have considerable experience with DBMS packages, like Oracle, Ingres, DB2, FoxPro, and OS/2 Data Manager.

My academic training has included C and many languages in the Unix and Windows environments as well as numerous programming assignments, working individually or as part of a team. With competence in Unix, C, SAS, Pascal, and a variety of other programming languages, I am comfortable in SUNOS, DOS, and VAX operating systems. I have used a variety of graphics, spreadsheet, database, desktop publishing, word processing, and telecommunication applications. I believe that my analytical skills and experience would contribute to the design department of Any Corporation.

I look forward to hearing from you.

Sincerely,

Chris Smith

Chris Smith

178 Green Street
Franklin Park, IL 60131
(312) 555-5555

June 28, 2001

Pat Cummings
Operations Manager
Any Company
1140 Main Street
Skokie, IL 60076

Dear Mr. Cummings:

Is Any Company in need of a hardworking and intelligent consultant/management specialist with over ten years' experience? If so, please consider the following qualifications.

For the past eight years, I have been actively involved in developing and administering health and welfare funds and defined contribution plans. I have also developed, designed, and implemented medical practice systems. This proficiency has been applied to both union and company requirements. My professional background is supported by a Master of Business Administration, Employee Benefits Specialist Certification, and current candidacy for a Master of Science in Computer Information Systems.

I hope to hear from you if I possess what you are looking for.

Sincerely,

Chris Smith

Chris Smith

"COLD" LETTER TO A POTENTIAL EMPLOYER
Editorial Assistant

178 Green Street
New York, NY 10020
(212) 555-5555

March 13, 2001

Pat Cummings
Personnel Director
Any Corporation
1140 Main Street
Chicago, IL 60605

Dear Ms. Cummings:

I would like to inquire about entry-level editorial openings with Any Corporation.

I am a senior at New York University, due to graduate this May with a Bachelor of Arts in Journalism and a minor in both Economics and English Literature. I am proficient in Word and WordPerfect and am familiar with PC and Macintosh operating systems. I currently work as a research intern for the economics division of Tradewinds Publishing in Newark.

I hope to hear from you if you have a position available.

Sincerely,

Chris Smith

Chris Smith

"COLD" LETTER TO A POTENTIAL EMPLOYER
Elementary School Teacher

178 Green Street
Lubbock, TX 79408
(806) 555-5555

July 7, 2001

Pat Cummings, Ph.D.
Superintendent
Any Public School
1140 Main Street
Chickasha, OK 73023

Dear Dr. Cummings:

I will be relocating to Chickasha this summer and would like to inquire about elementary teaching positions for September in the Any Public School system.

As you will note from my resume, I hold a Bachelor of Arts in Elementary Education. My professional training and experience began with the Rockford public school system, as a student teacher and substitute teacher. I have been employed as a fourth-grade teacher at Franklin Elementary School in Lubbock, where one of my projects was formulating a proposal for a high-ability learning program. The program was subsequently implemented, showed impressive results, and received favorable comment from both parents and students. Enclosed is an article I wrote describing the program that appeared in *Elementary Education* last August.

While at Franklin, I also took primary responsibility for selecting educational software for a new computer system and instructing the teaching staff in its use. The computers turned out to be a big hit with students, who took every opportunity to use them and the software. Again, parents were pleased with the improvement their children showed.

I look forward to hearing from you if you have an opening for someone with my qualifications.

Thank you for your consideration.

Sincerely,

Chris Smith

Chris Smith

"COLD" LETTER TO A POTENTIAL EMPLOYER
Financial Consultant

178 Green Street
Clinton, MS 39058
(601) 555-5555

May 8, 2001

Pat Cummings
Manager, Accounts Receivable
Any Corporation
1140 Main Street
Florence, MS 39073

Dear Ms. Cummings:

As a credit and collections consultant, I have been instrumental in substantially improving accounts receivable management, cash flow control, and the reduction of bad debt risk for a rapidly growing high-tech company.

Because of my performance during the past twelve years as staff accountant, credit analyst, credit and collection manager, and consultant, I was continually retained by new management during several acquisitions, mergers, and consolidations. These positions have provided me with increasingly responsible experience and challenge. However, due to the planned move of my function to Canadian headquarters, I am investigating new consulting opportunities with companies that can benefit from my expertise as a credit and collection specialist to improve their cash position.

I am confident of my ability to set up and manage credit and collection systems, procedures and controls, and employee training programs that will have the same positive results as experienced by my current employer.

I would appreciate the opportunity to discuss your credit/collection problems and my ability to come up with solutions without alienating your customer base. I hope to hear from you.

Sincerely,

Chris Smith

Chris Smith

"COLD" LETTER TO A POTENTIAL EMPLOYER
Fundraiser

178 Green Street
Winter Park, FL 32789
(407) 555-5555

June 1, 2001

Pat Cummings
Staff Coordinator
Any Organization
1140 Main Street
Orlando, FL 32809

Dear Ms. Cummings:

I would like to inquire about fundraising opportunities at Any Organization.

My experience in nonprofit development, public relations, and especially fundraising would be a strong asset to your organization. I have spent over three years as development and public relations assistant at the Women's Educational Society. My experience has encompassed preparing grant proposals, compiling program books for fundraising events, writing correspondence for the executive director, contributing to the quarterly newsletter, and generating donation acknowledgments. In addition, I am solely responsible for the fundraising database program in my office. This includes updating and maintaining donor records, generating daily income reports and financial analyses, and training staff and volunteers in data entry procedures.

I am involved with the production of two yearly appeals, and I write and edit the employee newsletter. In addition, as a member of the Executive Committee for my alumni class at Rollins College, I produce a quarterly newsletter with news from over fifteen hundred classmates. I am Macintosh and PC literate and taught myself desktop publishing to produce this newsletter.

Enclosed please find a resume and a copy of my employee newsletter and program book as writing samples.

Thank you for your consideration. I look forward to hearing from you.

Sincerely,

Chris Smith

"COLD" LETTER TO A POTENTIAL EMPLOYER
Human Resources Professional

178 Green Street
Grenvil, NE 68941
(402) 555-5555

October 19, 2001

Pat Cummings
Staff Coordinator
Any Corporation
1140 Main Street
St. Louis, MI 63130

Dear Ms. Cummings:

I am writing regarding opportunities your firm may have for an experienced human resources professional.

I have a solid track record as a human resources generalist working in a fast-paced environment with a reputable professional services firm in the Omaha area. I have successfully provided staff planning, recruiting, and employee relations support for several of the firm's key high-technology practices, which provide systems engineering and management consulting services. In addition, I have more than six years of solid accomplishment as a management analyst, systems analyst, and environmental management consultant providing technical and management services to both government and commercial clients.

I am seeking new and challenging responsibilities in an organization that would benefit from my background and specific mix of skills. I am willing to relocate and/or travel for the right opportunity.

Perhaps we could meet to discuss available openings at Any Corporation? Thank you for your time and consideration.

Sincerely,

Chris Smith

Chris Smith

"COLD" LETTER TO A POTENTIAL EMPLOYER
Legal Assistant

178 Green Street
Kankakee, IL 60901
(815) 555-5555

April 16, 2001

Pat Cummings
Director of Human Resources
Any Law Firm
1140 Main Street
Chicago, IL 60611

Dear Mr. Cummings:

I would like to inquire about a possible opening for a legal assistant at Any Law Firm.

In addition to a Comprehensive Certificate in Paralegal Studies and a Bachelor of Science in Business Administration, I have over five years' experience as a consumer mediator with the Attorney General's office. I have over seven years' comprehensive business experience, working and negotiating with senior-level management and decision-makers at Fortune 500 corporations. I have experience in all aspects of office support, with a typing speed of 75 wpm. I am a good writer and communicator and a fast study.

I look forward to hearing from you if my qualifications meet your needs.

Yours sincerely,

Chris Smith

Chris Smith

"COLD" LETTER TO A POTENTIAL EMPLOYER
Librarian

178 Green Street
Boston, MA 02215
(617) 555-5555

December 28, 2001

Pat Cummings
Director, Personnel
Any Library
1140 Main Street
Cambridge, MA 02138

Dear Mr. Cummings:

I am an experienced researcher who has worked extensively with archival records and secondary sources. Currently, I am seeking an opportunity to apply my research skills to a full-time position as a librarian.

My training has emphasized the importance of precise organization and the thoughtful use of evidence to make clear historical arguments, and my work in the Library of Congress, the Boston Public Library, and the Hauptstaatarchiv Stuttgart has shown me the usefulness of these skills in an actual research environment. As a librarian and as a consultant at Boston University, I have gained valuable experience supervising staff members, working directly with students and professors, and instructing departments on new reference procedures. I have also have experience with word processing and automated library reference networks.

I look forward to hearing from you if you have an opening for a librarian.

Thank you for your consideration.

Sincerely,

Chris Smith

Chris Smith

"COLD" LETTER TO A POTENTIAL EMPLOYER
Manager

178 Green Street
Kingsport, TN 37660
(901) 555-5555

January 11, 2001

Pat Cummings
Director of Human Resources
Any Corporation
1140 Main Street
Yukon, MO 65589

Dear Mr. Cummings:

I would like to inquire about any openings for a departmental manager at Any Corporation.

In my six years at Kimco, I was responsible for directing and coordinating the activities of accounting and support personnel in a $10 million manufacturing operation. I concurrently managed the cutting room and handled the purchase of approximately $5 million in raw materials, supplies, and capital equipment.

This position required entrepreneurial skills and the ability to manage varied responsibilities in a small, active manufacturing operation. While I was departmental manager, the company increased profits and was able to expand its staff by 15 percent.

I would appreciate the opportunity to discuss my qualifications further.

Thank you for your consideration.

Sincerely,

Chris Smith

Chris Smith

"COLD" LETTER TO A POTENTIAL EMPLOYER
Marketing Director

178 Green Street
Ada, OK 74820
(405) 555-5555
csmith@netmail.com

January 2, 2001

Pat Cummings
Director of Recruiting
Any Corporation
1140 Main Street
Sandy Springs, SC 29677

Dear Mr. Cummings:

It takes a seasoned marketing professional to provide the leadership, motivation, and strategies to introduce new products, develop profitable territories, and direct a productive and profitable organization in marketing. I have the experience and skills to build a sound customer base for your firm and would like to present my qualifications for your review.

I offer extensive marketing experience, including twenty years as director of marketing for a multimillion-dollar sportswear manufacturer. This position required successfully establishing new markets and major contacts regionally and nationally. During my time in that position, I secured thirteen long-term contracts with national retail chains.

If you feel that my qualifications would benefit your firm, I hope you will give me the opportunity to discuss them with you further.

Thank you for your consideration.

Yours sincerely,

Chris Smith

Chris Smith

"COLD" LETTER TO A POTENTIAL EMPLOYER
Mutual Funds Broker

178 Green Street
Honolulu, HI 96813
(808) 555-5555

April 14, 2001

Pat Cummings
Controller
Any Corporation
1140 Main Street
Chicago, IL 60611

Dear Mr. Cummings:

I am writing to inquire about employment opportunities as a broker within Any Corporation.

I have been involved in sales and business for twenty years. On "Black Monday," I solidified a $1 million lease in the largest mall in the West and then consummated the agreement during one of the worst economic scares since the Depression of the 1930s. I am the only private broker to raise construction money from Warga Property Investors, the top-grossing real estate trust in the world.

I am a highly motivated and principled professional who knows that her energy level, expertise, and commitment to success will produce results. I hope you will give me the opportunity to discuss my qualifications with you further.

Thank you for your consideration.

Sincerely,

Chris Smith

Chris Smith

"COLD" LETTER TO A POTENTIAL EMPLOYER
Printer

178 Green Street
Athens, GA 30601
(404) 555-5555

May 29, 2001

Pat Cummings
Manager, Production Department
Any Corporation
1140 Main Street
Atlanta, GA 30340

Dear Ms. Cummings:

My interest in a position in printing or related areas of graphic arts prompts me to forward my resume for your review.

During the past six years I have been employed with a major insurance company, where I rapidly advanced from an entry-level position to operator of a Xerox 9900 printing system. This experience, combined with my formal education in graphic arts, college-level courses in business administration, and experience in various areas of retail business operations, has equipped me with a sound background.

I will be in Atlanta from July 27 to August 3 prior to permanent relocation and wonder if it would be possible to arrange for an interview?

I look forward to hearing from you.

Sincerely,

Chris Smith

Chris Smith

"COLD" LETTER TO A POTENTIAL EMPLOYER
Public Relations Assistant

178 Green Street
Wheatland, ND 58079
(701) 555-5555

September 10, 2001

Pat Cummings
Vice-President, Human Resources
Zepf, Costigan, and Nardizzi
1140 Main Street
Los Angeles, CA 90053

Dear Ms. Cummings:

I would like to inquire about the possibility of a position as a public relations assistant with Zepf, Costigan, and Nardizzi.

In addition to my degree in Journalism and Public Relations, I have four years' experience with a modeling/talent agency and a modeling school. In both the teaching and model recruitment/placement environments, I have worked with key accounts in areas where image building and high visibility for client services or products was the ultimate objective. These activities also included selecting and placing models for television commercials. I have the skills to coordinate creative programs and innovative functions involving clients and the general public, and feel confident I could successfully apply my experience to a position in your firm.

I will be in Los Angeles at the end of the month and wonder if it would be possible to arrange for an interview?

Thank you for your consideration.

Sincerely,

Chris Smith

Chris Smith

178 Green Street
Fort Worth, TX 76114
(817) 555-5555

March 17, 2001

Pat Cummings
Director, Mental Health Services
Any Center
1140 Main Street
Dallas, TX 75206

Dear Ms. Cummings:

My involvement with a number of local counseling centers has given me the opportunity to become familiar with Any Center's work. My observation of your facility and its staff has confirmed my desire to join your organization in a counseling or group leader capacity.

For the past fifteen years, my experience has ranged from mental health aide to peer counselor and group leader working with alcoholics, drug abusers, and the mentally and emotionally disabled. I have extensive experience in alcohol and substance abuse counseling and providing related health-care services. I am also a candidate for a master's degree in Counseling/Psychology

I would very much like to speak to you about the possibility of joining your staff.
Thank you for your consideration.

Yours sincerely,

Chris Smith

Chris Smith

"COLD" LETTER TO A POTENTIAL EMPLOYER
Television Production Assistant

178 Green Street
Hilo, HI 96720
(606) 555-5555

June 24, 2001

Pat Cummings
Production Director
Any Television Station
1140 Main Street
Honolulu, HI 96822

Dear Ms. Cummings:

I would like to inquire about an entry-level production position at Any Television Station.

This May I graduated from the University of Hawaii-Hilo, with a Bachelor of Arts in Communications. Throughout my education, I have taken relevant broadcast communication courses dealing with production, writing, and research. I was also actively involved in the university newspaper. My duties entailed researching events and local talent, conducting interviews, and writing articles for the entertainment section of the paper.

Last summer, I worked as an intern for KBZT-TV's "Island Beat." I had the opportunity there to co-produce a local talk show, which required strong organizational and interpersonal skills. I pre-interviewed and scheduled guests for the show, handled financial and transportation details, and researched show topics. I also networked resource organizations to locate potential guests and panel members.

I will be in Honolulu the week of July 1 and wonder if it would be possible to schedule an interview?

Thank you for your consideration.

Sincerely,

Chris Smith

Chris Smith

BROADCAST LETTER
Chiropractor

178 Green Street
Chicago, IL 60601
(312) 555-5555

April 9, 2001

Pat Cummings
Chairperson of the Board
Any Clinic
1140 Main Street
Chicago, IL 60601

Dear Mr. Cummings:

I am a certified chiropractor currently exploring affiliations with established clinics. I have worked in the Chicago area for over twenty years and, as a result, my reputation for quality care is well known.

Currently, I work as a chiropractic therapist with the Chicago Chiropractic Center, a position I have held for the past fifteen years. In this capacity I provide spinal manipulation and handle necessary musculoskeletal needs of sports injury patients, alleviate pain in elderly and work-related patients, and assist the industrial-accident-injured in regaining strength and stamina.

I am also an active member of the American Chiropractic Association, Illinois Chiropractic Society, Chicago Chiropractic Society, and Sports Injury Council of the American Chiropractic Association.

I look forward to hearing from you if my qualifications are of interest to you.

Sincerely,

Chris Smith

Chris Smith

BROADCAST LETTER
Credit Manager

178 Green Street
Dickinson, ND 58601
(701) 555-5555

May 10, 2001

Pat Cummings
President
Any Corporation
1140 Main Street
Jamestown, ND 58405

Dear Mr. Cummings:

I am seeking a position as credit manager, to which I bring twenty years of successful credit management experience.

During the past ten years, as credit manager with a $20 million manufacturing and distribution firm, I have successfully set up and enforced credit controls, resulting in reducing DSO from 60 days to 33. I am continually involved in training personnel in credit and collection policies and procedures, troubleshooting and resolving sales and customer disputes, and making credit and collection decisions to reduce bad debt risk and increase cash flow.

Based on my contribution to the credit profession, I received recognition, through NACM New England, as Credit Executive of the Year in 1997 and was elected the first woman president of the same professional credit association for the 1998–99 term.

I look forward to hearing from you if you have a suitable position available.

Thank you for your consideration.

Sincerely,

Chris Smith

Chris Smith

BROADCAST LETTER
Freight Supervisor

178 Green Street
Raleigh, NC 27611
(919) 555-5555

September 1, 2001

Pat Cummings
District Supervisor
Any Corporation
1140 Main Street
Fayetteville, NC 28302

Dear Ms. Cummings:

During the past thirteen years, I have been actively involved in positions as field manager of container operations and night operations supervisor of freight stations and service centers, dealing with domestic and international freight deliveries.

In addition to supervising day-to-day operations, my experience encompasses hiring, training and supervising drivers, office and support personnel, and providing cost-effective, quality service within a multiple service network. I have sound knowledge of computer systems for freight movement management and am skilled in both troubleshooting and resolving problems relative to the movement of materials.

I would welcome the opportunity to discuss your requirements and further outline my qualifications.

Thank you for your consideration.

Sincerely,

Chris Smith

Chris Smith

178 Green Street
Cedar Rapids, IA 54201
(319) 555-5555

April 10, 2001

Pat Cummings
Chief Account Executive
Any Corporation
1140 Main Street
Wichita, KS 67202

Dear Ms. Cummings:

I am a seasoned marketing and sales executive seeking an association with an aggressive young firm like Any Corporation. I offer extensive experience and achievements in marketing, business development, and product management at national and international levels.

During the past ten years, some of my successes include the following:

- Developing sales programs and new businesses to increase penetration, market share, and revenue, using advanced, technically sophisticated systems-management services
- Participating in development and marketing teams for new service products for a service business generating $3.7 billion worldwide
  Assuming P&L responsibility for an added-value services business generating $90 million
- Establishing a record for producing positive bottom-line results in a high-tech, service-oriented business with worldwide markets

I am well qualified to direct areas that are key to achieving your business objectives. If you have such a position open, I look forward to hearing from you.

Sincerely,

Chris Smith

Chris Smith

178 Green Street
Tulsa, OK 74117
(918) 555-5555

August 12, 2001

Pat Cummings
Director
Any Company
1140 Main Street
Anadarko, OK 73005

Dear Ms. Cummings:

As a program manager interested in establishing connections with a new, up-and-coming firm, I submit the enclosed resume for your review.

My qualifications include over twelve years' managing experience with Ricochet Data. In this capacity, I developed and coordinated short- and long-range plans for designing and introducing four new microcomputers. I also created master charts to track major milestones and critical-path activities, directed a management task force to develop a set of work instructions for introducing outsourced products, and reduced product time to market by 25 percent.

My work in retail management might also be of interest to you. While employed at Lorenz Company, I generated gross annual sales in excess of $2 million for four consecutive years, managed a sales and service team of twenty people, and provided superior customer service and support.

Should my qualifications match your current or anticipated needs, I hope to hear from you.

Sincerely,

Chris Smith

Chris Smith

178 Green Street
Bridgeton, MO 63044
(314) 555-5555
csmith@netmail.com

January 3, 2001

Pat Cummings
President
Any Bank
1140 Main Street
St. Louis, MO 63146

Dear Ms. Cummings:

I am currently senior vice president at Central St. Louis Bank, where I have been employed for the past twenty-five years. Please note my credentials:

- Fifteen years of diverse experience, ranging from acting branch manager and district manager to my present position
- Supervision of all internal departments, including sales and account development, human resources, customer relations and customer service supervision, and product and sales support
- Responsibility for an increase in new business by 25 percent in one year through extensive interface with clients, decision-makers, and support personnel

Although my present position is challenging, I am interested in a position that addresses both national and international banking markets.

I look forward to hearing from you if you have such a position available.

Sincerely,

Chris Smith

Chris Smith

178 Green Street
Hazelwood, MO 63042
(606) 555-5555

July 18, 2001

Pat Cummings
Director
Any Employment Agency
1140 Main Street
Bridgeton, MO 63042

Dear Ms. Cummings:

The enclosed resume outlines my diverse experience in accounting and finance management. I am in search of an appropriate opportunity in the greater Missouri area.
The following are some of the strengths and capabilities I bring to a position:

- Solid understanding of financial statement preparation and review
- Proficiency at budget preparation and written analysis
- Proven ability to organize department goals to meet overall corporate goals
- Competence in resource management, both people and systems
- Strong leadership qualities, including motivating staff

I would welcome the opportunity to meet with you to discuss my background and credentials.
Thank you for your consideration.

Sincerely,

Chris Smith

Chris Smith

LETTER TO AN EMPLOYMENT AGENCY
Bookkeeper

178 Green Street
Kunia, HI 96759
(808) 555-5555

July 17, 2001

Pat Cummings
Partner
Any Employment Agency
1140 Main Street
Honolulu, HI 96813

Dear Mr. Cummings:

If one of your clients is in need of a highly motivated bookkeeper who can handle the day-to-day details necessary to insure smooth operation, I would appreciate your consideration of my enclosed resume.

During the past nine years, I have been employed in a variety of industries, including manufacturing, distribution, property management, retail, and automotive services. I have gained diverse experience in accounting, bookkeeping, administration, office maintenance, and customer service. I have sound knowledge of credit policies and collection procedures to control accounts receivable and loss reduction while retaining good customer relations and business.

Although my preference is to stay on the Pacific Coast, I would consider relocation based upon salary, benefits, and future opportunity for growth. My present salary is $38,000.

I am most interested in the opportunities available with your client base and hope to hear from you to arrange a meeting.

Sincerely,

Chris Smith

Chris Smith

LETTER TO AN EMPLOYMENT AGENCY
Claims Processor

178 Green Street
Tarrytown, NY 10591
(914) 555-5555

December 4, 2001

Pat Cummings
Employment Specialist
Any Employment Agency
1140 Main Street
Bronx, NY 10474

Dear Mr. Cummings:

My interest in securing a position of claims processor with one of your client companies has prompted me to forward my resume for your review.

In addition to six years of experience as home health aide, inpatient claim representative, and, since 1999, medical assistant with Marifield Rehabilitation Hospital, I have sound knowledge of medical terminology, procedure codes, and medical office systems, including related computerized applications. I have an associate degree in Sociology, graduated as medical assistant, and am currently a candidate for an associate degree in Nursing.

Thank you for your consideration.

Sincerely,

Chris Smith

Chris Smith

LETTER TO AN EMPLOYMENT AGENCY
Cook

178 Green Street
Sioux Falls, SD 57117
(605) 555-5555

April 5, 2001

Pat Cummings
Director
Any Employment Agency
1140 Main Street
Dayton, OH 45402

Dear Mr. Cummings:

I will be moving to the Dayton area next month and would like to submit my qualifications for any suitable opportunities available through your agency.

I am an accomplished cook with experience in a wide variety of food service institutions, including restaurants, catering services, and banquet functions. My areas of expertise include all aspects of food preparation, from ordering ingredients to presentation.

As you can see from my enclosed resume, I most recently worked as a rounds cook at the McGuiness Inn. In addition to cooking to order, I performed several supervisory duties, including scheduling shifts, controlling inventory, and resolving problems.

I will be visiting Dayton to secure housing during the week of April 15 and would be available to meet with you or a client during that time.

Thank you for your consideration.

Sincerely,

Chris Smith

Chris Smith

LETTER TO AN EMPLOYMENT AGENCY
Dental Assistant

178 Green Street
Lafayette, IN 47902
(317) 555-5555

May 3, 2001

Pat Cummings
Associate
Any Employment Agency
1140 Main Street
Indianapolis, IN 46225

Dear Mr. Cummings:

I am a trained dental assistant with several years of both clinical and administrative experience. I am conducting a job search for a full-time position in the Indianapolis area and have heard about your agency's placement record through several acquaintances. I would appreciate any assistance your agency could provide me in securing such a position.

My qualifications are as follows:

- Over six years of experience as a dental assistant, contributing to direct patient care and patient relations
- Honor graduate as a dental assistant from National Education Center
- Sound knowledge of medical terminology and clinical procedures
- Certified in first aid, cardiopulmonary resuscitation, and electrocardiography
- Additional experience as receptionist/secretary with an executive search/management consulting firm, a financial management company, and realty firms

My compensation requirement is in the mid-twenties.
I look forward to hearing from you.

Sincerely,

Chris Smith

Chris Smith

LETTER TO AN EMPLOYMENT AGENCY
Executive Assistant

178 Green Street
Mobile, AL 36625
(203) 555-5555

July 18, 2001

Pat Cummings
Associate
Any Employment Agency
1140 Main Street
Birmingham, AL 25202

Dear Ms. Cummings:

I am an experienced executive/administrative assistant seeking appropriate career opportunities in the corporate arena.

In addition to five years of staff experience at Bradstreet and Associates, I have worked for three years as executive assistant to the president and to the executive vice-president of a software development company. In that capacity, my responsibilities included a variety of assignments, both independent and with team projects, writing and typing executive correspondence, and other administrative activities. My word processing and spreadsheet expertise includes Word, Lotus 1-2-3, and Excel, and my technical background enables me to quickly develop expertise in other such applications.

Thank you for your consideration. I look forward to hearing from you.

Sincerely,

Chris Smith

Chris Smith

178 Green Street
Jacksonville, FL 32203
(904) 555-5555

August 7, 2001

Pat Cummings
Partner
Any Employment Agency
1140 Main Street
Tallahassee, FL 32302

Dear Mr. Cummings:

I have recently relocated to Florida and would like to be considered for a court or legal-related administrative position with your clients.

In Washington, I was office manager for a respected court reporting firm. My job responsibilities required organization, attention to detail, writing, and significant computer skills. I have extensive experience working on multiple projects and meeting deadlines in a team-oriented environment. As a result, I have developed strong time management and interpersonal skills.

I look forward to hearing from you.

Thank you for your time.

Sincerely,

Chris Smith

Chris Smith

178 Green Street
La France, SC 29656
(803) 555-5555
csmith@netmail.com

March 30, 2001

Pat Cummings
Associate
Any Employment Agency
1140 Main Street
Spartanburg, SC 29304

Dear Mr. Cummings:

If one of your clients is in need of a reliable, competent, well-organized individual for their office management staff, I have the qualifications and dedication for the position.

During the past ten years, I have held progressively responsible positions in office management with manufacturing, distribution, export, and service companies. I have broad experience with manual and automated accounting and administrative systems, customer service, personnel supervision, event and meeting planning, credit and collection, and executive support. I function best in a diverse, busy environment and have established a reputation for being organized and capable of coordinating and handling multiple assignments cost-effectively and to schedule.

Should you know of any suitable opportunities, I would appreciate your informing me. I look forward to hearing from you.

Sincerely,

Chris Smith

Chris Smith

178 Green Street
Phoenix, AZ 85012
(602) 555-5555

January 15, 2001

Pat Cummings
Director
Any Employment Agency
1140 Main Street
Keyport, WA 98101

Dear Ms. Cummings:

I will be relocating to your area next month and would be interested in a position in which to apply my chemical, electromechanical, and mechanical skills. I would be a good match for a progressive, technically oriented company seeking support in research, manufacturing, or production.

During the past fifteen years, I have held progressively responsible and sophisticated positions with RHG Corporation, including automated manufacturing machine operator, research and development assistant, and senior laboratory technician. I am skilled in all trades and have more than six years' experience managing and supervising fleet maintenance for cars and trucks. I have additional training in accounting, real estate, supervision, and management, and am considered an expert in automotive and general mechanics.

Do you know of any openings that match my qualifications?

I look forward to hearing from you.

Sincerely,

Chris Smith

Chris Smith

LETTER TO AN EMPLOYMENT AGENCY
Property Manager

178 Green Street
Salamanca, NY 14779
(716) 555-5555

May 13, 2001

Pat Cummings
Director
Any Corporation
1140 Main Street
Chicago, IL 60605

Dear Mr. Cummings:

In July I will be relocating to the Chicago area. I am forwarding the attached resume to see if you can assist me in locating a position as a property manager with an orientation to sales.

I have two years' direct experience, involving all aspects in the management of 275 apartments and four commercial units in three buildings. My responsibilities include a range of activities, from advertising and promotion of apartments to competitive analysis of rate structures.

My experience also includes contractor negotiations, liaison with government and service agencies, personnel relations, financial management, and other functions basic to the effective management of complex properties.

Thank you for your consideration.

Sincerely,

Chris Smith

Chris Smith

LETTER TO AN EMPLOYMENT AGENCY
Sales/Customer Service Representative

178 Green Street
Trenton, NJ 08619
(609) 555-5555

November 4, 2001

Pat Cummings
Employment Representative
Any Employment Agency
1140 Main Street
Linwood, NJ 08221

Dear Mr. Cummings:

I am writing to inquire if your agency might be able to assist me in my search for a position in either sales or customer service.

As you can see from my enclosed resume, I have over seven years' experience in positions including sales assistant, claims investigator, and bank teller. Some of my applicable skills include:

- Acting as liaison between customers, staff, and management
- Investigating and resolving customer requests and problems
- Tracking and expediting sales orders; ascertaining order accuracy
- Processing a wide range of financial transactions; maintaining accuracy and balance

I would be interested in discussing any employment opportunities you feel would be applicable to my skills. I am willing to travel and would be interested in a salary in the $35,000 range.

Thank you for your consideration.

Sincerely,

Chris Smith

Chris Smith

LETTER TO AN EMPLOYMENT AGENCY
Security Guard

178 Green Street
Minden, NV 89423
(702) 555-5555

May 4, 2001

Pat Cummings
Director
Any Employment Agency
1140 Main Street
Las Vegas, NV 89125

Dear Mr. Cummings:

Having recently moved to the Las Vegas area, I would greatly appreciate your assistance in securing a position as a security guard.

For the past eight years, I have worked as a security guard. At the Willow Mead Art Museum, in Wyoming, my duties included patrol, surveillance, and control of facilities and areas. I also maintained reports, records, and documents as required by administration.

For the past three years as a bank security guard, I was responsible for ensuring the safety and security of customers, bank employees, and bank assets. My compensation for that position was in the high $20,000 range.

I look forward to finding a similar position through your agency. I can begin working immediately.

Sincerely,

Chris Smith

Chris Smith

LETTER TO AN EXECUTIVE SEARCH FIRM
Director of Information Services

178 Green Street
Idaho Falls, ID 83415
(208) 555-5555
csmith@netmail.com

August 15, 2001

Pat Cummings
Executive Recruiter
1140 Main Street
Boise, ID 83706

Dear Mr. Cummings:

During our meeting at the Minority Professional Recruiting Center on July 22, we discussed opportunities with your client firms that are of great interest to me.

I am currently seeking a challenging environment where I can apply my combined technical knowledge, experience, and ability to create and implement innovative concepts for greater information systems efficiency. My qualifications include the following:

- Thirteen years of experience with MIS corporate information systems
- Experience in operating and supervising administrative functions of several UNIX systems
- Skill in communicating with domestic and international networks, mainframes, and network system support
- Ability to work as a team member, team leader, and/or independent contributor, working offsite via modem and data network, to assist users in sales, finance, manufacturing, and production
- Ability to generate positive results in a company's information systems and networks by streamlining systems and improving user training and performance

I have enclosed a resume and would appreciate meeting with you to discuss my qualifications. Relocation is not a problem, and my compensation requirements are in the low $70,000 range.

Thank you for your consideration.

Yours sincerely,

Chris Smith

Chris Smith

LETTER TO AN EXECUTIVE SEARCH FIRM
Management Consultant

178 Green Street
Gusher, VT 84030
(802) 555-5555

April 1, 2001

Pat Cummings
Executive Recruiter
Any Corporation
1140 Main Street
Chicago, IL 60605

Dear Mr. Cummings:

I have played a key role in designing, implementing, reorganizing, and managing a variety of functions—including operations, manufacturing, materials, engineering, and quality assurance—for nationally and internationally recognized corporations.

Currently, I am seeking a position with a company that can benefit from my twenty years of progressively responsible management experience in the above areas. My expertise is diverse and includes the following:

- Five years as director of operations for a $60 million manufacturer
- Over six years as materials manager with a multiplant, multiwarehouse, $10 million manufacturer of industrial rubber products
- Over nine years as manufacturing coordinator with a toy manufacturer, with responsibilities related to expansion of existing manufacturing and support facilities, setup of new facilities, manpower planning, union relations, and capital equipment investment and materials purchases

Should you know of any opportunities for someone with my background, I would greatly appreciate your consideration.

Yours sincerely,

Chris Smith

Chris Smith

LETTER TO AN EXECUTIVE SEARCH FIRM
Operations Manager

178 Green Street
Minnetonka, MN 55343
(612) 555-5555

March 23, 2001

Pat Cummings
President
Any Search Firm
1140 Main Street
Minneapolis, MN 55408

Dear Ms. Cummings:

Based on my diverse background and experience with high-end, midrange, and low-end hardware, software, and network products, I feel that I can make a valuable contribution toward new product planning, market development, and expansion for a firm within your client base.

My experience over the last seventeen years has required the ability not only to develop and market packaged and customized software for many industries in domestic and international markets, but also to provide the support products for end-users at all levels. Because of this diversity, I am easily able to transfer my skills to marketing other products.

In addition to a strong marketing and sales background, I have also established a record for setting up, staffing, and managing top-producing, profitable district offices.

Should you be aware of an advanced marketing and development position in the $80,000-$90,000 range, please consider my qualifications.

Thank you for your consideration.

Sincerely,

Chris Smith

Chris Smith

178 Green Street
Madison Heights, MI 48071
(313) 555-5555

July 18, 2001

Pat Cummings
President
Any Search Firm
1140 Main Street
Detroit, MI 48239

Dear Mr. Cummings:

During the past ten years, I have held positions ranging from production supervisor to plant and operations manager with a $16 million manufacturer and importer of electrical products. I am seeking a new position where I can contribute to a company's cost-effective, quality operation and profitability.

In my current position as plant manager, I developed a stable workforce and environment following a restructuring. Under my direction, the company has benefited from efficient supervisory staff and support personnel in all phases of plant operations, including production, purchasing, inventory control, warehousing, distribution, and maintenance of a 325,000-square-foot facility.

I would welcome the opportunity to apply my proven track record to one of your client firms. Relocation is not a problem. My compensation requirements are in the $70,000-$80,000 range.

Thank you for your consideration.

Sincerely,

Chris Smith

Chris Smith

178 Green Street
Concord, NH 03302
(603) 555-5555

July 20, 2001

Pat Cummings
Executive Recruiter
1140 Main Street
New York, NY 10022

Dear Mr. Cummings:

I believe that the varied accounting, finance, and general management experience I have gained over the course of my career may be of interest to you in your current or anticipated client searches.

As a seasoned, certified accountant, I have successfully managed general ledger, cash accounting, accounts payable, employee disbursements, and fixed asset operations. As a manufacturing plant controller, I managed the accounting activities and general administrative functions of a $35 million manufacturing plant.

My qualifications include the following:

- Preparing, analyzing, and presenting P&L, balance sheet, departmental expense, manufacturing variance, and other operating reports
- Preparing $2 million annual departmental operating budgets, analyzing results, initiating required operational improvements, and preparing forecasts
- Developing annual strategic and operational improvements, resulting in a 15percent increase in efficiency
- Overseeing human resources, purchasing, payroll, and other plant administrative functions
- Maintaining quality accounting operations by implementing internal controls testing programs

I have also managed the interface between my group and the data center running my applications, directed the MIS professionals that supported my applications, and managed the enhancement projects that steadily improved day-to-day operations.

While my prime interest is securing a position on the East Coast, I am willing to relocate for the right opportunity and compensation ($85,000–$95,000).

Thank you for your consideration.

Sincerely,

Chris Smith

Chris Smith

CHAPTER 12

Networking Letters

NETWORKING LETTER
Administrative Assistant

178 Green Street
Durango, CO 81301
(719) 555-5555

November 16, 2001

Pat Cummings
Attorney at Law
Any Firm
1140 Main Street
Pueblo, CO 81001

Dear Mr. Cummings:

Recently, Luke Gokey suggested I contact you concerning any assistance you might be able to provide with my job search. I am interested in joining an organization in a position that would use my legal, administrative, and managerial knowledge and experience.

As indicated on my resume, my law-related background is extensive and varied. For twelve years, I have supervised records and staff activities within the Any County Registry of Deeds. Unfortunately, I have reached the plateau of responsibility level within the structure of this position and am now seeking to continue in my career.

I am especially interested in a legal administrative position, preferably with a private firm or corporation. I am willing to relocate and/or travel.

Should you know of any related openings or contacts to whom I should pass my resume, I would appreciate your calling me.

Thank you for your time.

Sincerely,

Chris Smith

Chris Smith

NETWORKING LETTER
Auto Salesperson

178 Green Street
Brooklyn, NY 11201
(718) 555-5555

December 2, 2001

Pat Cummings
Regional Manager
Any Corporation
1140 Main Street
Rochester, NY 14623

Dear Ms. Cummings:

During a recent visit to Rochester, my longtime friend Bill Atwood mentioned your name as a contact in the field of auto sales. I understand that your corporation has contracted Bill's agency several times to promote your regional dealerships. I would like to take this opportunity to ask for any assistance you might be able to provide with my job search.

Due to recent downsizing, I am seeking a new, long-term association with an aggressive, fast-paced dealership. During the past eight years, my positions have ranged from salesperson to sales manager with a high-volume dealership. My expertise is in developing, training, motivating, and managing a top-producing sales team in a highly competitive market. I am an effective communicator, with presentation skills designed to generate results when dealing with management, personnel, and the general public. I have established and continually maintained a record of achievement as Salesperson of the Month and Salesperson of the Year for generated sales and margin of profit.

I will be visiting the Rochester area next week and would like to meet with you if your schedule permits it. Your insight into the market and the future of the industry, as well as any specific advice or contact names, would be very helpful. I will call your office next Monday to see if we can find a convenient time to meet.

Thank you for your consideration.

Sincerely,

Chris Smith

Chris Smith

178 Green Street
St. Louis, MO 63130
(314) 555-5555

June 8, 2001

Pat Cummings
Vice-President, Operations
Any Bank
1140 Main Street
Omaha, NE 68124

Dear Mr. Cummings:

Jennifer Mills, a colleague of mine at United Bank in St. Louis, mentioned your name as an authority in the Midwest banking industry. Jennifer met you on a visit to your Omaha office last month and was impressed by both the reputation and successful operation of your branches. I am writing to ascertain any information you can provide regarding banking opportunities in the Omaha area, where I will be relocating next month.

As my resume indicates, I am a skilled professional with over ten years of relevant experience. In addition to an MBA degree (Executive Program —five years' field representative experience required), and a BA degree in Economics and Finance, I have more than eighteen years of comprehensive banking experience. My expertise includes all aspects of banking and finance, credit administration, and management, including commercial lending and development, real estate loans, and end-to-end joint venture management. My experience also encompasses a term as chief financial officer for a Japanese-American joint venture, and a term as vice president, Bank of St. Louis.

I will be visiting Omaha next week to begin my job search. Would your schedule permit a few moments to speak with me at that time?

Thank you.

Sincerely,

Chris Smith

Chris Smith

NETWORKING LETTER
Chief Financial Officer

178 Green Street
El Paso, TX 79998
(915) 555-5555
csmith@netmail.com

June 25, 2001

Pat Cummings
President
Any Bank
1140 Main Street
Menomonie, WI 54751

Dear Ms. Cummings:

I am currently seeking a position as a chief financial officer. Brad Peltser suggested that I contact you to focus my job search. I am exploring the Midwest as a site for relocation and am anxious to learn more about the Midwestern job market.

I have a record of outstanding success in managing corporate financial operations for fast-paced manufacturing companies and associated commercial operations, in multilocation, multistate, and international environments.

My sixteen years of progressively responsible experience has encompassed management of all aspects of financial and treasury functions, from cost accounting manager to chief financial officer and vice president, finance. This experience includes managing corporate real estate, human resources, and general operations. In addition to holding an M.B.A. in Finance and a B.A. in Accounting, I have been a Certified Public Accountant since 1985.

May we meet? I would appreciate your advice about the job market in the Midwest for senior-level officers.

Thank you for your consideration.

Sincerely,

Chris Smith

Chris Smith

NETWORKING LETTER
Customer Support Representative

178 Green Street
Scranton, PA 18510
(717) 555-5555

April 1, 2001

Pat Cummings
Customer Support Manager
Any Corporation
1140 Main Street
Greenburg, PA 15601

Dear Ms. Cummings:

I am a former college classmate of your son Dennis, and have, since graduation, worked as a customer support representative for a manufacturer of high-volume copier and reprographic equipment. Although my position has been challenging and fast-paced, at this point in my career, I am seeking a new position where my expertise and motivation can be more fully applied.

I had lunch with Dennis last week while on a business trip to Pittsburgh, and he suggested that you might have an opening within the customer support department of your corporation.

During the past three years, I have gained progressively responsible experience in providing sales support and training to new hires and end-users of major commercial, institutional, industrial, and government accounts on a national level. I am an effective representative and support individual with the ability to provide liaison between sales, service, customers, and corporate personnel.

I wonder if we could meet so that I can further outline my qualifications and how I could contribute successfully to your firm?

I look forward to hearing from you.

Sincerely,

Chris Smith

Chris Smith

NETWORKING LETTER
Editor

178 Green Street
Arlington, VA 22207
(703) 555-5555
csmith@netmail.com

December 9, 2001

Pat Cummings
Vice-President, Editorial
Any Corporation
1140 Main Street
Wise, VA 24293

Dear Ms. Cummings:

John Curran, whom I saw recently at the ABA convention, spoke highly of your creative, market-sensitive approach to publishing and your tremendous success in publicizing your books. He also said you might have plans to expand your editorial team and suggested that I write you.

I have seven years' experience as a nonfiction editor. For the past two years, I have acquired books for McDoogle's Professional Book Group. I work with authors on books that address the wide range of challenges facing today's managers and small-business owners. I also acquire books on personal business topics for the career/self-help market, like Margaret Miller's *Loving Your Job*. A January 2002 release, Miller's book has already received a strong response from book clubs (20,000-copy advance order) and an enthusiastic endorsement from Michael Morin.

Earlier in my career, I acquired books on health, fitness, recreation, and other nonfiction topics for Stevens & Dunn. Although designed for the academic environment, these books had strong crossover appeal to the trade market. I have also procured many author contacts and book ideas I would like to pursue.

I wonder if we could meet to discuss the possibility of an opening at Any Corporation?

Thank you.

Sincerely,

Chris Smith

Chris Smith

178 Green Street
Downers Grove, IL 60515
(708) 555-5555

January 25, 2001

Pat Cummings
Human Resource Director
Any Bank
1140 Main Street
New York, NY 10128

Dear Ms. Cummings:

John Monroe, of First Avenue Bank, informed me that you might be expanding your staffing needs. Based on my comprehensive experience in the field of finance, I can offer your firm a broad range of management and administrative skills in banking.

During the past twenty-five years, I have played a key role in the trust banking industry, in positions ranging from tax officer to my current position as chief trust officer. Because of my ability to adapt strategies to changing conditions, I was able to apply innovative approaches that increased productivity, accuracy, and profits. This substantially improved our customer service, corporate visibility and image, and customer base.

I am confident I could contribute my expertise to the continued success of Any Bank and would welcome the chance to discuss career opportunities.

Thank you for your time.

Sincerely,

Chris Smith

Chris Smith

178 Green Street
Kilgore, TX 75662
(903) 555-5555

January 16, 2001

Pat Cummings
Finance Manager
Any Corporation
1140 Main Street
Austin, TX 78713

Dear Mr. Cummings:

It was a pleasure meeting you last month while visiting Bob and Cheryl Maxmillian at their home in Austin. As you may recall, at that time I was working as international controller of Divinex, a multidivision manufacturer of automatic test equipment. Recent ownership changes have prompted me to seek another position in finance management. When I updated Bob on my search recently, he suggested I obtain your assistance.

I possess over sixteen years of experience working with foreign manufacturing entities and sales and service subsidiaries, which has involved corporate financial planning and analysis, international reporting, treasury and tax management, and interactive MIS systems for both corporate and divisional financial operations.

Should you know of any corporations in the Austin area in need of someone with my qualifications, would you kindly forward my resume to the appropriate contacts? Also, I will be visiting Bob and Cheryl in two weeks, to meet with industry insiders and continue my search. Should your schedule permit, I would like to meet, perhaps for lunch or dinner. I would appreciate your input as a fellow professional in the field. I will contact you next week to find a time that is good for you.

Thank you for your assistance. I hope to see you again soon.

Sincerely,

Chris Smith

Chris Smith

NETWORKING LETTER
Marketing Assistant

178 Green Street
Dazey, ND 58428
(701) 555-5555

June 2, 2001

Pat Cummings
Director of Marketing
Any Corporation
1140 Main Street
Chicago, IL 60605

Dear Mr. Cummings:

It was a pleasure talking to you during our flight to Rome last April. I hope you enjoyed your trip!

As you may recall, I was a senior at Harvard University studying marketing and sales. You were kind enough to give me your business card with instructions to contact you once I was "liberated from the fetters of academia." Finally, that day has arrived.

Although I am a recent graduate, I have held several internships at major Boston corporations. As a result, I know how to buy and sell in an aggressive, no-holds-barred manner while retaining the diplomacy necessary to garner respect.

I have enclosed my resume for your reference and file. If you know of anyone seeking a fresh addition to their marketing team, please let me know.

Thank you for your help.

Sincerely,

Chris Smith

Chris Smith

NETWORKING LETTER
Marketing Specialist

178 Green Street
Youngstown, OH 44555
(216) 555-5555

March 23, 2001

Pat Cummings
Director, Sales and Marketing
Any Corporation
1140 Main Street
Largo, MD 20772

Dear Ms. Cummings:

Thank you for taking the time to speak with me after your sales presentation on behalf of Any Corporation last Thursday. As you may recall, I am relocating to your area next month and am currently in search of a marketing position within Any Corporation.

During the past five years, my experience in my present position as marketing specialist has been focused on product management, strategic planning, marketing, and the sale of equipment, systems, chemicals, and related products and services. I am responsible for the worldwide marketing of bio-instrument chemicals sold to biotech markets, pharmaceutical markets, and research laboratories.

As my enclosed resume indicates, my success in product management, new business and market development, and sales management of national and international markets has provided me with qualifications I feel would contribute to the growth and profitability of your firm.

At your convenience, I would like to discuss, in detail, the mutual benefit of my joining your management team. I consider myself to be a persistent achiever and feel confident that I can make a significant difference.

I appreciate your consideration and look forward to speaking with you.

Yours sincerely,

Chris Smith

Chris Smith

178 Green Street
Conway, AR 72032
(501) 555-5555

April 4, 2001

Pat Cummings
Chief Loan Officer
Any Bank
1140 Main Street
Little Rock, AR 72203

Dear Mr. Cummings:

Recently I ran into an old college roommate and friend, Ellen Barie. As I am currently considering a new position with a bank or corporation as a mortgage or loan officer, Ellen suggested I contact you. She mentioned that she had worked as a teller at your Little Rock main branch and thought you might be interested in someone with my qualifications.

As the enclosed resume indicates, my extensive loan experience has encompassed office supervision and general bookkeeping within the mortgage, insurance, and banking industries, concentrating in credit and collections. My current position as a senior collections specialist has provided me with the opportunity to accomplish and exceed a set objective of reducing delinquent loans from $24 million to $10 million within six months. At this point, I feel I have successfully surpassed both company and personal goals and am searching for new and greater challenges.

I am quite interested in the opportunities available at Any Bank. Could we meet for a personal interview?

I look forward to hearing from you.

Sincerely,

Chris Smith

Chris Smith

NETWORKING LETTER
Nurse

178 Green Street
Kingston, RI 02881
(401) 555-5555

November 19, 2001

Pat Cummings
Nursing Director
Any Hospital
1140 Main Street
Bristol, RI 02809

Dear Ms. Cummings:

Are you in need of a nursing professional with extensive clinical, research, and teaching experience? Laura Fogerty, a nurse in your pediatric unit, suggested I contact you regarding employment opportunities at Any Hospital.

I have fifteen years' experience in clinical research and direct patient care, with an emphasis on neuroscience intensive care, memory disorders, and brain and cognitive sciences. During the past three years, I have functioned as a staff nurse with duties in a neuro intensive care unit.

I am well qualified to teach, counsel, conduct utilization reviews, or administer programs related to health care, equipment, or human services—all in appropriate settings. I am capable of making presentations to individuals and groups, am skilled at conducting meetings and teaching classes, and have the required communication skills to demonstrate as well as instruct medical professions and support staffs.

I look forward to hearing from you if a suitable opening is available at Any Hospital. Thank you for your consideration.

Sincerely,

Chris Smith

Chris Smith, R.N.

178 Green Street
Hayward, CA 94541
(805) 555-5555

June 6, 2001

Pat Cummings
Office Manager
Any Corporation
1140 Main Street
Los Angeles, CA 90017

Dear Ms. Cummings:

I received your name as a contact for my job search from a mutual friend, Steve Herson. I was employed at Steve's bank several years ago and worked closely with him on several projects. In a recent conversation, Steve mentioned that you might be in need of a professional with my qualifications.

As my resume indicates, in addition to a Bachelor of Arts in Economics, my background encompasses eleven years of progressively responsible and sophisticated hands-on experience, ranging from marketing research assistant to union benefits coordinator and human resources administrator. In my present position as payroll administrator with a special emphasis on the day-to-day details of financial operations and related areas, I have gained experience in organization and operations.

I look foward to hearing from you. Thank you for your consideration.

Sincerely,

Chris Smith

Chris Smith

178 Green Street
Arlington, VA 22229
(703) 555-5555

July 22, 2001

Pat Cummings
Director of Operations Management
Any Corporation
1140 Main Street
Macon, GA 31201

Dear Ms. Cummings:

As Alex Drumlins may have informed you, I was caught in Timony's recent downsizing. I am writing to inquire if Any Corporation has any openings in production or operations, or if you may know of any industry contacts.

As you can see from my resume, my experience extends throughout the last two decades. In addition to a B.S. in Management, I possess four years of supervisory and production management experience with a large, Washington, D.C.-based corporation.

Thank you for your consideration.

Sincerely,

Chris Smith

Chris Smith

NETWORKING LETTER
Publicist

178 Green Street
Woodland Hills, CA 91367
(213) 555-5555
csmith@netmail.com

July 9, 2001

Pat Cummings
Publicity Director
Any Corporation
1140 Main Street
Santa Ana, CA 92701

Dear Mr. Cummings:

Lee Cyndis suggested I write you with regard to support areas of advertising and public relations. I would appreciate any information or advice you can provide about how to search for a publicity-related support position. I have enclosed a resume to acquaint you with my background.

I possess comprehensive experience in the support of direct mail fundraising for a major university. My training and expertise also include publicity and public relations, staff training and supervision, program coordination, budget management, market research, copyediting, and management and administration of related detail.

I have excellent writing skills, work well under pressure, and meet deadlines consistently. In addition, I have experience with streamlining operations for enhancing production efficiency at optimum cost.

I look forward to hearing from you.

Thank you for your time.

Sincerely,

Chris Smith

Chris Smith

178 Green Street
Daytona Beach, FL 32117
(904) 555-5555

January 24, 2001

Pat Cummings
Production/Operations Manager
Any Corporation
1140 Main Street
Long Grove, IL 60047

Dear Mr. Cummings:

I enjoyed talking with you on the plane from Denver. I only wish we had met a little earlier, on the slopes of Winter Park. Enclosed is the resume you asked to see. I am interested in discussing opportunities within Any Corporation.

As a quality control engineer, I played a key role in the growth of Victor, Inc., where I interfaced with all departments, including sales, purchasing, manufacturing, and inventory. I am knowledgeable in quality functions and have experience bringing product lines through the transitional stages from research and prototype to full production.

During the past seven years, I implemented and audited clean room contamination control, electrostatic discharge, and internal auditing programs for semiconductor and engineering facilities.

I will be in Chicago for a training conference from April 10 to April 17 and would enjoy meeting with you at that time to talk further. Please let me know if this would be a good time to schedule a meeting.

I look forward to hearing from you.

Sincerely,

Chris Smith

Chris Smith

178 Green Street
Birmingham, AL 35294
(205) 555-5555

November 15, 2001

Pat Cummings
Personnel Director
Any Corporation
1140 Main Street
Mobile, AL 36630

Dear Ms. Cummings:

Maureen Deegan suggested I speak with you regarding a secretarial position with Any Corporation. I hope, in reviewing my background, you will find that my qualifications suit your needs.

During the last five years with Stuart Photographers, my responsibilities have included assisting on shoots, handling incoming calls, arranging appointments, and light typing. As service representative for the Dalton Corporation, I dealt with all customer inquiries and resolved problems in shipping and billing. I am accustomed to working closely with staff and management in a fast-paced environment and enjoy the satisfaction of doing a job well.

I look forward to hearing from you if a position is available at Any Corporation.

Sincerely,

Chris Smith

Chris Smith

NETWORKING LETTER
Staff Accountant

178 Green Street
Newport, RI 02840
(401) 555-5555

November 12, 2001

Pat Cummings
Director, Career Services
Any College
1140 Main Street
Smithfield, RI 02917

Dear Ms. Cummings:

It was a pleasure meeting you at the alumni luncheon last Monday, and kind of you to offer your assistance in my job search. I would greatly appreciate any assistance you could provide.

During the past three years, I have been employed as a staff accountant with Acme Corporation, with responsibility for maintaining financial statements and monthly closings and preparing financial reports using Lotus 1-2-3. During the prior four years, while attending college, I held positions part-time of increasing responsibility in areas ranging from auditing to accounts payable in corporate and nonprofit environments.

If you know of any corporation in need of an experienced accountant, I would appreciate your letting me know.

Thank you for your help.

Sincerely,

Chris Smith

Chris Smith

178 Green Street
Savage, MT 59262
(406) 555-5555
csmith@netmail.com

September 26, 2001

Pat Cummings
Telecommunications Consultant
Any Corporation
1140 Main Street
Chicago, IL 60605

Dear Ms. Cummings:

Several years ago, I was your son Dan's classmate at the University of Miami. When I bumped into him last week in Billings, Montana, of all places, he informed me that you deal closely with several leading specialists in the telecommunications field and suggested I contact you immediately.

I am interested in joining a company where I can contribute strong skills and education in communications. My qualifications are as follows:

- A Bachelor of Arts in Communications
- Familiarity with all areas of marketing, public relations, and advertising
- One year's experience as a promotions intern at a radio station
- Fluency in German

I would greatly appreciate any advice or referrals you might be able to provide. I will call you in a few days to follow up.

Thank you for your time.

Sincerely,

Chris Smith

Chris Smith

NETWORKING LETTER
Telemarketer

178 Green Street
Wooster, OH 44691
(216) 555-5555

December 4, 2001

Pat Cummings
Director, Telemarketing
Any Corporation
1140 Main Street
Columbus, OH 43216

Dear Mr. Cummings:

Your name was given to me by Leanne Marquis, who I understand has worked with you on several promotional projects. Leanne is a close friend of my mother's and has been very helpful in assisting me obtain an entry-level position in telemarketing. Leanne felt that I would benefit from your extensive industry experience.

I possess four years of successful part-time and full-time employment in sales administration and support. I have worked most recently in telemarketing, direct mail, marketing, and sales for a variety of product or service-oriented companies.

Any referrals or advice you could provide for my job search would be greatly appreciated. I will contact your office on Friday morning to see if I could schedule a few moments at your convenience.

Thank you for your consideration.

Sincerely,

Chris Smith

Chris Smith

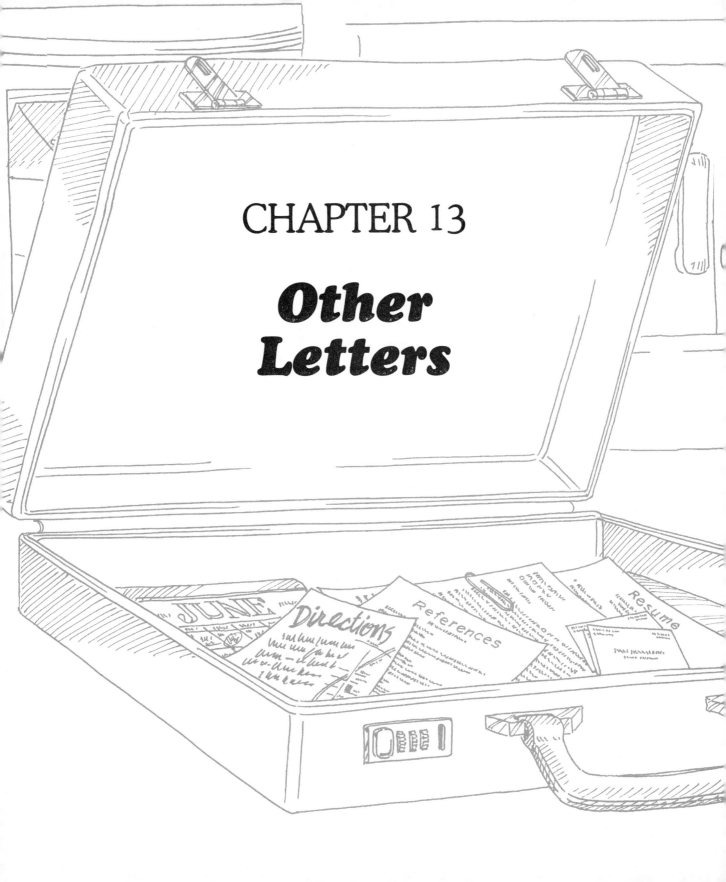

CHAPTER 13

Other Letters

178 Green Street
Norfolk, VA 23510
(703) 555-5555
csmith@netmail.com

February 14, 2001

Pat Cummings
Director of Human Resources
Any Corporation
1140 Main Street
Casper, WY 82604

Dear Ms. Cummings:

Thank you for taking the time from your schedule on Friday to speak with me regarding available COBOL programmer positions.

As you can see from my resume, my hardware exposure has included Suzuki and HyTech, and I have had substantial experience in implementing both batch and online computer systems using COBOL. Each position I have held has led to advancement and the assumption of greater responsibilities.

I appreciate your time and consideration. I look forward to hearing from you.

Sincerely,

Chris Smith

Chris Smith

178 Green Street
Boise, ID 83725
(208) 555-5555

August 3, 2001

Pat Cummings
Vice-President
Any Corporation
1140 Main Street
Chicago, IL 60605

Dear Mr. Cummings:

I am forwarding my resume with regard to the opening we discussed in your marketing department.

Although I am currently employed in a management position, I am interested in a career change, especially one where I can combine a thorough knowledge of boating with my sales, marketing, and communication skills. I am an imaginative, well-organized self-starter with a strong interest in boating. As a semiprofessional sailboat racer, I twice won national honors and participated in the races at Cape Cod. In addition, I have made lasting contacts with owners and officials. I am confident that my business background and knowledge of boats would enable me to have a favorable impact on both your sales and image.

Thank you for your attention. I look forward to speaking with you again.

Sincerely yours,

Chris Smith

Chris Smith

178 Green Street
Baldwyn, MS 38824
(601) 555-5555
csmith@netmail.com

August 28, 2001

Pat Cummings
Manager, Billing Department
Any Corporation
1140 Main Street
Jackson, MS 39217

Dear Mr. Cummings:

Thank you for a most enjoyable interview in reference to the computer operator position at Any Corporation. It was a pleasure meeting you and Robert Richmond and learning more about the operations of your billings department.

I am interested in contributing my seven years of experience operating computer systems to the success of your firm. Per your suggestion, I will call your office next week to check the status of the hiring process.

Again, thank you for your time and consideration.

Sincerely,

Chris Smith

Chris Smith

178 Green Street
West Hazelton, PA 18201
(717) 555-5555

July 18, 2001

Pat Cummings
Hiring Manager
Any Corporation
1140 Main Street
Pittsburgh, PA 15222

Dear Mr. Cummings:

It was a pleasure to meet you and Joyce Duncan last Friday and learn more about the products and services provided by Any Corporation. The executive assistant position sounds like the ideal opportunity to apply my administrative and organizational skills to the overall operations of your firm.

As I mentioned, the qualifications I would bring to the position include the following:

- Nine years' experience handling all office functions, including preparing and generating letters and reports, payroll, accounts payable and receivable, and customer service
- Organizational proficiency, reflected in my revamping of a records storage system at Quicksilver Metro to reduce records access time by over 60 percent from the previous system
- Scrupulous attention to detail, which led me to discover and correct over $125,000 in duplicated and incorrectly assigned labor charges
- Experience working with a variety of software applications, including Word, WordPerfect, Excel, and Lotus1-2-3

Thank you for considering my candidacy. I look forward to hearing from you.

Sincerely,

Chris Smith

Chris Smith

178 Green Street
Washington, DC 20016
(202) 555-5555

November 11, 2001

.

Pat Cummings
Bookkeeper
Any Corporation
1140 Main Street
Washington, DC 20001

Dear Mr. Cummings:

    Thank you so much for your great reference regarding my application for the bookkeeping position at The Baldwin Company.

    I have since been offered, and have accepted, the position. I appreciate your efforts on my behalf.

Sincerely,

Chris Smith

Chris Smith

178 Green Street
Hobbs, NM 88240
(505) 555-5555

May 31, 2001

Pat Cummings
Account Manager
Any Corporation
1140 Main Street
Santa Fe, NM 87504

Dear Mr. Cummings:

I appreciate the kind letter of recommendation you wrote to assist me in my job search. Yesterday, I received an offer to begin work as a staff accountant with Enstel and Yang. Your praise of my internship work at Any Corporation definitely contributed to my success.

If there is anything I can do in return, please contact me.

Thank you again.

Sincerely,

Chris Smith

Chris Smith

178 Green Street
Twodot, MT 59085
(406) 555-5555
csmith@netmail.com

October 14, 2001

Pat Cummings
Managing Editor
Any Press
1140 Main Street
Chicago, IL 60605

Dear Ms. Cummings:

I am happy to inform you that I have just accepted an offer for employment as an acquisitions editor at Dandelion Publishing Group. I should begin work there the first week of November.

I would like to thank you for all your help during my job search, specifically for putting me in touch with Ninona Punder at Dandelion's Billings office.

If there is ever anything that I can do in return, please don't hesitate to contact me. Yours was a favor I shall not soon forget.

Again, many thanks and best wishes.

Sincerely,

Chris Smith

Chris Smith

178 Green Street
Downers Grove, IL 60515
(708) 555-5555

May 12, 2001

Pat Cummings
Occupational Therapist
Any Rehabilitation Center
1140 Main Street
Evanston, IL 60201

Dear Ms. Cummings:

Thank you for taking the time to meet with me on Friday. I enjoyed meeting with you and learning about the programs offered at Any Rehabilitation Center.

Our discussion definitely strengthened my interest in occupational therapy as a career path. I am planning to take your advice and enroll in a graduate program in September. In the interim, I will contact the referrals you provided to inquire about summer internship possibilities.

Thank you again for your assistance.

Sincerely,

Chris Smith

Chris Smith

178 Green Street
Dunnellon, FL 34433
(813) 555-5555

November 14, 2001

Pat Cummings
President
Any Corporation
1140 Main Street
Fort Lauderdale, FL 33301

Dear Ms. Cummings:

In a recent letter, David Kipler, group vice president with your company, indicated that my resume and letter regarding employment with Any Corporation were being forwarded for your review. Not yet having had a response, I am enclosing the attached resume to reiterate my interest in becoming a member of your firm.

I offer seven years' experience and the qualifications that could be well applied in a managerial position with your firm. In addition to a master's degree in Business Administration, I offer experience in relevant positions ranging from product management trainee to clinical service manager of five company-operated outpatient treatment centers.

Thank you for your consideration. I look forward to hearing from you.

Sincerely,

Chris Smith

Chris Smith

RESPONSE TO REJECTION
Assistant Editor

178 Green Street
White Plains, NY 10604
(914) 555-5555
csmith@netmail.com

July 1, 2001

Pat Cummings
Editor
Any Publication
1140 West 43rd Street
New York, NY 10036

Dear Mr. Cummings:

I would like to thank you again for the chance to interview for the assistant editor position with Any Publication. Although I am disappointed I was not chosen, I enjoyed meeting with you and your staff and learning more about your company.

I am still interested in opportunities with Any Publication and would appreciate it if you would keep me in mind for future openings in either your magazine or book divisions.

Thank you again for your consideration.

Sincerely,

Chris Smith

Chris Smith

WITHDRAWAL FROM CONSIDERATION
Regional Sales Manager

178 Green Street
Kenilworth, NJ 07033
(201) 555-5555

July 1, 2001

Pat Cummings
Human Resources Director
Any Corporation
1140 Main Street
New Brunswick, NJ 08933

Dear Mr. Cummings:

As you may recall, I spoke with you over the phone several weeks ago regarding the status of my application for the regional sales manager position. While I understand that you are still in the process of sorting through resumes, I wanted to notify you that I have just accepted another offer for a similar position.

Thank you for the time you extended to inform me of the hiring process.

Sincerely yours,

Chris Smith

Chris Smith

REJECTION OF OFFER
Editor

178 Green Street
Bartow, FL 33830
(813) 555-5555
csmith@netmail.com

September 17, 2001

Pat Cummings
Senior Editor
Any Publishing Company
1140 Main Street
Miami, FL 33173

Dear Mr. Cummings:

Thank you for your offer of employment and for your confidence in my abilities as an editor.

As I explained during our phone conversation, a newly arisen personal situation has caused me to rethink my plans to relocate to Miami. After much deliberation, I have decided that I must postpone my plans. I apologize for informing you of this change on such short notice, and I regret not being able to accept the opportunity to work for such a distinguished organization.

Sincerely,

Chris Smith

Chris Smith

ACCEPTANCE LETTER
Underwriter

178 Green Street
Batavia, IL 60510
(708) 555-5555

October 16, 2001

Pat Cummings
General Manager
Any Insurance Agency
1140 Main Street
Decatur, IL 62526

Dear Mr. Cummings:

I received your letter dated October 14 and am pleased to accept your employment offer. I look forward to beginning work as an underwriter for such a prestigious organization.

I would like to confirm my start date of October 28. I have given notice to my current employer and expect a smooth transition to Any Insurance Agency.

Once again, I would like to thank you and Frank Russo for your positive response to my candidacy.

Sincerely,

Chris Smith

Chris Smith

178 Green Street
Shawnee Hills, OH 43965
(216) 555-5555

May 31, 2001

Pat Cummings
Research Scientist
Any Medical Association
1140 Main Street
Chicago, IL 60605

Dear Mr. Cummings:

I am writing to inform you that I have moved to the above address and telephone listing.
Enclosed is an updated copy of my resume for your files. I am looking forward to hearing
more about any laboratory assistant positions you may have available.

Thank you.

Sincerely,

Chris Smith

Chris Smith

178 Green Street
Houston, TX 75217
(713) 555-5555
csmith@netmail.com

March 17, 2001

Pat Cummings
President
Any Company
1140 Main Street
Addison, TX 75001

Dear Mr. Cummings:

   Regretfully, I must tender my resignation, effective April 1. Although I have enjoyed watching Any Company grow from its beginnings to its present formidable size in my capacity as marketing director, my ability to contribute to its future success is past. For this reason, I have accepted a position with a smaller company that offers the potential for growth.

   I am grateful for the experience. If there is anything I can do to make my departure a smooth one, please let me know.

Sincerely,

Chris Smith

Chris Smith

Index

We Have

EVERYTHING!

Available wherever books are sold!

Everything **After College Book**
$12.95, 1-55850-847-3

Everything **Astrology Book**
$12.95, 1-58062-062-0

Everything **Baby Names Book**
$12.95, 1-55850-655-1

Everything **Baby Shower Book**
$12.95, 1-58062-305-0

Everything **Barbeque Cookbook**
$12.95, 1-58062-316-6

Everything® **Bartender's Book**
$9.95, 1-55850-536-9

Everything **Bedtime Story Book**
$12.95, 1-58062-147-3

Everything **Beer Book**
$12.95, 1-55850-843-0

Everything **Bicycle Book**
$12.95, 1-55850-706-X

Everything **Build Your Own Home Page**
$12.95, 1-58062-339-5

Everything **Casino Gambling Book**
$12.95, 1-55850-762-0

Everything **Cat Book**
$12.95, 1-55850-710-8

Everything® **Christmas Book**
$15.00, 1-55850-697-7

Everything **College Survival Book**
$12.95, 1-55850-720-5

Everything **Cover Letter Book**
$12.95, 1-58062-312-3

Everything **Crossword and Puzzle Book**
$12.95, 1-55850-764-7

Everything **Dating Book**
$12.95, 1-58062-185-6

Everything **Dessert Book**
$12.95, 1-55850-717-5

Everything **Dog Book**
$12.95, 1-58062-144-9

Everything **Dreams Book**
$12.95, 1-55850-806-6

Everything **Etiquette Book**
$12.95, 1-55850-807-4

Everything **Family Tree Book**
$12.95, 1-55850-763-9

Everything **Fly-Fishing Book**
$12.95, 1-58062-148-1

Everything **Games Book**
$12.95, 1-55850-643-8

Everything **Get-a-Job Book**
$12.95, 1-58062-223-2

The ultimate reference for couples planning their wedding!

- Scheduling, budgeting, etiquette, hiring caterers, florists, and photographers
- Ceremony & reception ideas
- Over 100 forms and checklists
- And much, much more!

$12.95, 384 pages, 8" x 9¼"

Personal finance made easy—and fun!

- Create a budget you can live with
- Manage your credit cards
- Set up investment plans
- Money-saving tax strategies
- And much, much more!

$12.95, 288 pages, 8" x 9¼"

For more information, or to order, call 800-872-5627 or visit www.adamsmedia.com/everything

Adams Media Corporation, 260 Center Street, Holbrook, MA 02343

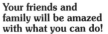

From the publishers of this book

CareerCity.com

Search *4 million* job openings at all the leading career sites with just one click!

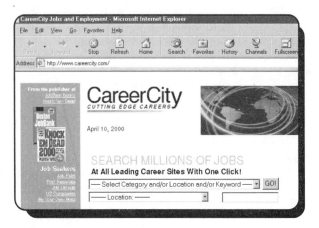

Find all the great job openings without having to spend hours surfing from one career site to the next.

Now, with just one click you can simultaneously search all of the leading career sites . . . at CareerCity.com!

You can also have jobs come to you! Enter your job search criteria once and we automatically notify you of any new relevant job listings.

Plus! The most complete career center on the Web including . . .

- Descriptions and hot links to 27,000 U.S. companies
- Comprehensive salary surveys in all fields
- Expert advice on starting a job search, interviews, resumes and much more

You'll find more jobs at CareerCity.com!

Post your resume at CareerCity and have the job offers come to you!

It's fast, free, and easy to post your resume at CareerCity—and you'll get noticed by hundreds of leading employers in all fields.